School Organization and Administration

Published by
Saurabh Publishing House

SCHOOL ORGANIZATION AND ADMINISTRATION

Dr. K. C. Nayak

Saurabh
Publishing House
4735/22, Prakash Deep Building,
Ansari Road, Daryaganj, New Delhi - 110002

Published by :
SAURABH PUBLISHING HOUSE

Distributed by :
LOTUS PRESS Publishers & Distributors
Unit No. 220, Second Floor, 4735/22, Prakash Deep Building, Ansari Road,
Daryaganj, New Delhi - 110002
Ph : 23280047, 32903912, 098118-38000
E-Mail : lotus_press@sify.com

Saurabh Publishing is an imprint of
Lotus Press Publishers & Distributors

School Organization and Administration

ISBN : 978-81-89005-89-4 (H/B)

Printed in India by Concept Imprint, Delhi

Preface

One of the essential characteristics of successful school management is its flexible character. The manager should be dynamic, not static: it should provide enough scope for additions and alterations. The rules and regulations should act as a means to an end and not an end in themselves. Dead uniformity and mechanical efficiency is the very antithesis of good administration. The framework of administration should provide enough scope to the administrator to help the needy student, and, the needy teacher, to change the time schedule to suit the weather to meet any emergency. A word of caution here. Flexibility does not mean that the administration should be in a fluid condition without any specific norm or standard rules and regulations, creating confusion and chaos at every step. What is meant is a proper balance between rigidity and elasticity.

The school management must not be a bundle of theoretical principles, but must provide practical measures to achieve the desired objectives. Whatever objective is decided it must be achievable and practicable to avoid frustration. There must be close connection between school management and the social and political philosophy of a country. It must adjust itself to the impact of new ideals, new patterns and new mores of the society. In an autocratic country, educational theory and practice will have to be different from that of a democratic country because education is one of the means to achieve social and political objectives. Indian education is decentralized and democratized whereas Chinese education is characterized by regimentation due to political philosophies of the respective countries. In India, school administration has to be democratic because of politic democracy in the country.

This book deals with the topics of—*Basic Facts about School Management; Objectives of Education; Features and Principles of Educational Administration; Organization Models; Educational Planning and Difficulties; School Building and Arrangements; Position of Headmaster; Role of Teacher and Relationship; Planning Process; Training for Teachers; School Discipline and Punishment; Curriculum Development; Health Education and Medical Examination;* etc.

I hope that students and those in the education field will find it useful for academic and competitive examinations. I owe a deep sense of gratitude to my publisher for materializing my present endeavour.

Dr. K. C. Nayak

Contents

1

Basic Facts about School Management

School is the basal unit of the big hierarchy of educational administration. Today, as never before, India, needs educational institutions not only to guard its past but also to advance its future. "The destiny of India is now being shaped in the class-rooms"—this the assessment of situation by the first ever Comprehensive Commission (1964-66) on Indian Education. Schools are to be the first class nurseries for the education of children in democratic citizenship which India needs to make its democracy permanently viable. Efficient school administration is crucial to the success of democracy. Some theory and philosophy will have to be evolved for guiding the educational administration process at all levels and to be clear about the objectives so that we do not miss the targests.

SCOPE OF SCHOOL MANAGEMENT

The following may be considered as necessary components of school administration.

1. Providing the human equipment—headmaster, teaching staff, ministerial staff and menial staff.
2. Providing the material equipment such as building, furniture, farms, laboratories, library, museum, art gallery etc.

3. Preparing time-table.
4. Maintaining discipline.
5. Organization of library, museum, hostel etc.
6. Organization of health and physical education.
7. Organization of exhibitions and museums.
8. Preparing the curriculum for the different classes.
9. Organization of a systematic co-curricular programme.
10. Organization of guidance service.
11. Maintaining the school records.
12. Providing various auxiliary services like mid-day meals, school uniform, text-books etc.
13. Coordinating the work of home, school and community.
14. Supervision of school work.
15. Evaluation of student achievement.
16. Financing and budgeting.

In short, any thing and everything having to do something with the education of the child through the agency of the school, will be included in school management.

Objectives of School Management

1. To Reflect and Conserver Basic Values. "The unity of a culture consists in the fact that all valuations are mutually shared in some degree." Today, in America in the face of new, emerging values, and despite the rhetoric of "cultural pluralism", a cement of shared values binds individuals and groups to the commonwealth, to the national society.

As a social institution, school primarily reflects and conserves the values, norm, and practices of particular society: only secondarily, and then rarely, does in initiate change and innovation on its own.

2. To Carry out Educational Futures. Thus, educational futures are drawn mainly, and by implication from societal futures, on all levels from family, through state and nation, to planet. For example, Harry Broudy has suggested that the major future demand by society on schooling will be for vocational competence, civic competence, and humanness (*i.e.*, individuality, personhood, and freedom). Dwight Allen concluded that, "To get past (rigid prerequisities and lockstep credentialing)..., we need to implement nonlinearity, simultaneity, and random access to education by allowing students to learn what they want, when they want it, to make education self-directed, continuing, and enjoyable."

A growing number of educators have become interested in the study of educational futures, or as it is sometimes referred to, educational policy studies or policies research. Their forecasts vary, both in terms of the educational topics they choose to study and ill terms of their actual projections. Among the topics education futurists have selected for study and research are curriculum content (*i.e.*, knowledge, skills, values, and attitudes), materials and methods; school and curriculum organization patterns; patterns; preserves and in-service education of teachers, schemes for financing public, private, and parochial schools; teachers organizations or unions, and salaries and benefits; student demographic characteristics; educational media and technology; politics and control of education; global, international education; functions of non-school educative agents, such as publishers, commercial television, families, and community agencies; and school buildings and other learning environments.

Taking a broad perspective on education in the future, two general, long-term trends seem to pervade public education in every nation. These are:

(i) The tendency of systems of schooling to first maximize the number of persons served by the system, and then to maximize the quality of service to special client groups and to individual clients, and

(ii) The tendency of curricular and decision-making orientations to shift from local, to national, to worldwide concerns and arenas.

The historical pattern has survived for each level of public education—elementary, secondary, and higher—to grow toward serving a maximum number of potential students. This has been a progression "upward", saturating each level in turn.

Two other broad tendencies of educational systems are toward the centralisation of authority and power at "higher" levels from local school districts to state departments of education to central or national government; and the broadening orientation of curriculum from local to national and then to global dimensions.

3. To Manage Social Change. Changes continue to occur in society. Individuals never react with each other in the same way on any two occasions. In each of their contact, there it be called "social change" or transformation. It indicates the dynamic nature of society. The process of change in society is not simple. Society is a complex network or relationships, in which different members participate in different ways. With the change in relationships the behaviour changes. Men are daily faced with new situations. Behaviours, differ with each situation. Thus, social change may involve new techniques, new ways of living, developing new ideas and formulation of new values.

4. To Profit by Experience. Education implies profiting by experience. Learning is nothing but gaining through experience, when we think of educating the young we means providing them with such experience as may help them develop physically, mentally, morally, socially and culturally. Thus, education aims at an all-round development of individuals. The aim of education is not only to develop individuals, but to make them adjusting members of society and useful citizens.

5. To Propagate Science. Science involves search for truth. To find out truth, one has to develop a scientific attitude. It involves collection of data, analysis and synthesis of the information collected and drawing conclusion. Here again education plays an important role.

6. To Adopt Technology. Adoption of technology is the most urgent need of today's society. By technology is meant not only the science of industrial arts, but a systematic and science way of doing things. As the knowledge in various subject areas is increasing, new methods are being developed. Making use of the most novel technology in various fields of work and life, men can achieve best results.

7. To Carry out Modernization. Modernization does not merely change the material culture but affects values and way of life of society. The society is transformed from its backward structure to a forward-looking, progressive and prosperous set-up. In modernization, society makes full use of the discoveries and innovations in science and technology. It can tap natural resources for better living of its people. It recognizes the importance of cultural heritage but is not bound by the orthodoxy beliefs.

Modernization is a process in which man makes changes, but at the same time maintains his identity. In a sense, it is a process of outlook of man. In a world predominated by science, one cannot live without its benefits. Indian society is mostly influenced by art, culture and religions. There is yet only a little influence of science on it. Hence, there is a need for a tilt in educational facilities from art and culture to science and technology.

8. To Realize National Integration. Today anti-social elements raising their heads in society. The unity and integrity of the nation is threatened. Slogans of casteism or communalis, linguism, or regionalism rent the air. Besides *andolans, gheraos* and *destruction* of public property have become the order of the day. This disturbs peace and creates chaos. Under such circumstances, serial transformation for national integration is the urgent need. This too can be achieved through education only.

By organizing *sarva dharma prarthana,* community life activities, picnics and feasts Indian schools can sow the seeds of national unity in children. Besides, the school uniform too of the institutions cultural and social functions in the schools, help develop the feelings of national integration.

9. To Form Character. Social transformation for character formation is an urgent need. Today there is a death of national character m Indians. Corruption, bribery, blackmail, dishonesty and selfishness have taken hold of society, Indiscipline, in obedience and indulgence m destructive activities mark the psyche of the students. Given the circumstances, serious thought and attention has to be paid to character.

Here school can play an important role. Since childhood is a malleable phase of student life, the impression formed at this time become lasting. During this period efforts should be made to inculcate virtues like truth non-violence, sacrifice, love and tolerance m the minds of the children. The students of today will be the citizens of tomorrow and they will shoulder the responsibility of the nation.

Characteristics of Successful School Management

1. Flexibility. One of the essential characteristics of successful school management is its flexible character. The manager should be dynamic, not static: it should provide enough scope for additions and alterations. The rules and regulations should act as a means to an end and not an end in themselves. Dead uniformity and mechanical efficiency is the very antithesis of good administration. The framework of administration should provide enough scope to the administrator to help the needy student, and, the needy teacher, to change the time schedule to suit the weather to meet any emergency. A word of caution here. Flexibility does not mean that the administration should be in a fluid condition without any specific norm or standard rules and regulations, creating confusion and chaos at every step. What is meant is a proper balance between rigidity and elasticity.

2. Practicability. The school management must not be a bundle of theoretical principles, but must provide practical measures to achieve the desired objectives. Whatever objective is decided it must be achievable and practicable to avoid frustration.

3. Confirmity to the Social and Political Philosophy of the Country. There must be close connection between school management and the social and political philosophy of a country. It must adjust itself to the impact of new ideals, new patterns and new mores of the society. In an autocratic country, educational theory and practice will have to be different from that of a democratic country because education is one of the means to achieve social and political objectives. Indian education is decentralized and democratized whereas Chinese education is characterized by regimentation due to political philosophies of the respective countries. In India, school administration has to be democratic because of politic democracy in the country.

4. Successful Achievement of Desired Objectives. Successful management is one which leads to the successful achievement of desired objectives of education in a particular community *e.g.*, healthy social living, development of good physical, social, moral, intellectual and aesthetic qualities and healthy democratic living.

5. Efficiency. Successful management is that which results in maximum efficiency. This will be possible only when human and material resources are properly utilized—right man at the right place; right work at the right time, every activity and project is well planned and well executed.

School management must facilitate education. It exists for the pupil and its efficiency has to be measured by the extent to which it contributes to teaching and learning.

Principles of Democratic School Management

India happens to be the largest democracy in the world. To make democracy successful, we have to revitalize and recharge our schools to the full. Schools will be able to add tempo to the struggling democracy if the following principles are taken into consideration while administering them.

1. Democratic Philosophy of Education. In his Report on Indian Administration, Dr. Paul H. Appleby has emphasized the need for a philosophical but simple theory for administration for a country which is .determined to create a welfare state. If a philosophy is necessary for general administration, it is all die—more so for educational administration which is seeking to fashion a new pattern of education suited to the needs and aspirations of modern India. In an educational institution in a democracy, the administrator is a friend and a guide. He consults his colleagues, honours their opinions, confers with them in staff meetings, meets them informally in gatherings and clubs. He is one among the equals. He recognizes the worth of each individuals child, finds out his potentialities and gives him, help and guidance according to his requirements. Thus, the total managements becomes a joint show of the Headmaster, teachers, and pupils. Every body has a clear consciousness and realisation of the purpose of democratic philosophy with which the school is administered.

2. Student Centred. All educational management must be largely student-centred. The purpose of all educational endeavour is the walfare of the student. This 'flesh and blood' should never be lost sight of in the midst of facts, figures and files. Enough opportunities must be provided for the wholesome development of the students. Whatever is done in the school should be of the students, by the student and for the students.

3. Freedom. Enough freedom should be given to all to exercise their powers and talents. The power of critical thinking, an important requisite of democracy, can only be cultivated by individuals in an atmosphere of freedom. The Headmaster should give due recognition to any signs of display of resourcefulness on the part of teachers. They should be free to questions, offer constructive suggestions, conduct fresh experiments and bring about healthy changes. The pupils should also be allowed enough freedom to rise to the full stature of their abilities.

4. Flexible, Adaptable and Stable. Educational management must hold fast to the good, change what requires changing and be fertile in considering individual differences in all personalities involved.

Democracy can only become real through its educational institutions, which will teach its children the democratic way of life. There must pervade an atmosphere of justice, freedom, and cooperation in the educational institutions, only then good training in leadership and followership can be given.

Practical Measures for Democratic School Management

1. Staff Council. The aim of the staff council is to plan all important matters of the school. The staff council may be further split up into committees to plan and execute specific tasks. Meetings of the staff council should be held frequently to discuss all important issues. Senior members of the staff should constitute the staff council.

2. Student's Council. A student council consisting of Secretaries from different houses, associations and clubs should form a student's council with the aim of giving the students training in self-government. The student councils can be guided and assisted by a staff adviser.

3. Staff Meetings. Meetings of the staff should be called fortnightly to discuss the different matters and the staff should have the idea that whatever has been decided upon is mainly their work.

4. Special Committee of Students. In addition to the student council, special committees should be formed, duly elected by the students to carry out specific duties and organize special activities for maintaining discipline, organizing debates, dramatics, exhibitions 'flower shows literary societies, music concerts etc.'

5. Social Service Squads. Such type of squads can render service in the form of laying roads, arranging committee functions cleanliness campaigns in the neighbourhood, literary campaigns, helping the sick, looking after the families of the jawans, collection of national defence fund, etc.

***

2

Objectives of Education

In every walk of life, aims are of unique importance. Without fixing up aims, the work that we take up remains dull and cheerless aims. In fact it makes the process lively, and they also provide satisfaction at the end. In the field of education aims are very essential. Undoubtedly, education is a purposeful and planned activity. It makes a man quite fit for the society. Therefore, we should try to fix up aims in advance and then make efforts to achieve them.

Education without an aim is quite meaningless. In the words of John Dewey, "An aim is a foreseen end that gives direction to an activity or motivates behaviour." An aim to predetermined goal which inspires the welfare activities of an individual, after careful thinking and proper planning it is achieved. In fact, an aim is that predetermined goal which stimulates human activities to achieve it.

Basic Issues

1. They emerge out of the existing conditions.
2. They are tentative. They can be revised as per need and requirement.
3. They are well-defined.
4. They are flexible.
5. They are related to the life and aspirations of the people.

John Dewey suggested the following criteria for aims of education:

1. Good aims are related to real situations of life. They grow out of these situations and they can be achieved only under these situations.

2. A good aim represents a span of diverse activity. The real objective in pursuing an end is not the end itself but the course of the activity itself which constitutes the core of education.

3. Good aims are flexible. These should be flexible enough to meet the demands of changing circumstances of life.

There is a great importance of aims of education. All scholars philosophers and educationists have laid great stress on the importance of aims in education. Being a systematic and planned activity, education loses much of its significance without clear-cut aims. According to *Encyclopaedia of Modern Education,* "Education is purposeful and ethical activity. Hence, it is unthinkable without aims." In fact, without aims neither an individual nor an institution is capable of realizing its potentialities."

Educational aims are important due to the following reasons:

1. Aims are necessary as they give direction to an act. Education is a planned activity. It has certain aims in view. The aim as a foreseen end as it gives direction to the education process. Without aims, the educator is like a sailor who does not know his destination and the pupil is like a rudderless vessel which may be drifted along somewhere ashore.

2. Aims allow us to act intelligently. John Dewey has aptly remarked, "Acting with an aim is all one with,

acting intelligently." Thus by keeping the aim in view, one knows what one is doing and why one is doing it. It saves wastage of time and energy.

3. Aims are necessary for efficient school administration. They help the school authorities in organizing, equipping and managing the school. This refers to the selection of teachers, curriculum, planning, proper library equipment, planning of various activities etc. Each activity is guided by educational aims.

4. Aims help in assessing the outcomes of the education process. They are necessary because they help in measuring the success and failure of work done in the school.

5. Aims give direction to the work of the pupils. Once the pupils are clear about the aims, they are likely to co-operate and work with zeal for the achievement of these aims.

6. Aims give continuity and significance to education. Education is a continuous process. It has an intrinsic continuity. It is the aim that gives continuity and significance to the series of events and experiences that make up what we call education. So aims are potential seeds from which grows the plant of a well-defined educational policy. Aims help us in acting with meaning.

7. Aims are useful for parents and general public. Parents and general public can appreciate the work of the school in the light of aims. Aims put restraint on the undue criticism from the parents.

Aims are the core of a workable philosophy of education. Without philosophy, an educator could not have aims and without aims he could not have a practical philosophy.

Aims are an integral part of the fabric of the educative process. They enable an individual to continue his education. As such, an aim is not an end; it is only a means to an end.

Aims are both within and without the educative process. Ward G. Reader rightly points out, "Education finds its aims both within and without the educative process. It must be kept in mind the interests and the abilities of the pupil and prepare him to share in democratic living both now and when he becomes an adult."

Factors at Work

Many factors contribute to the determining of educational aims. These factors touch every phase of human life and also reflect socio-cultural trends. The following factors usually determine aims of education:

1. Philosophy of Life. Aims of education have direct relationship with the prevailing philosophy of life. Different thinkers and philosophical thoughts influence the course of education and its aims. Idealism emphasizes self-realization and divine perfection as the aims of education. According to the natural-view point, self-expression or self-gratification should be the aim of education. The pragmatic school of thought views life as the process of socialization of an individual. Similarly, existentialism, realism and other philosophical view points recommended their own aims of education.

2. Human Nature. Educational aims have often been decided keeping in view the human nature. Idealists regard 'unfolding the divine man' as the aim of education. To naturalists, the aim of education is "self-expression."

3. Religious Factors. Though there is no state religion in India, yet different religious view points influence the aims of education. The denominational institutions run by different religious organization shave to work to realize the goals accordingly.

4. Political Ideology. No system of education can rise above the political ideologies of the country. In other words, political ideologies influence aims of education in a significant way. According to Brown, "Education in any country and at points reflects value of the ruling class." Under a totalitarian system, the aims of education are different from those under a democratic political system.

Under a democratic setup, the—aims of education are flexible. The goal of education is the good man who is to be educated for life of freedom. Education aims at developing the full personality of each individual, irrespective of caste, creed, class or religion.

Under a totalitarian system, the aim of education is to propagate the state ideology. It is, in fact, indoctrination. The good of the individual lies in his working for the good of the state. Thus he dies for the state.

5. Cultural Factors. Socio-cultural heritage of a country largely determines the aims of education. Education has to preserve and develop the cultural heritage. The changing and developing pattern of culture directly influences the aims of education.

6. Socio-Economic Problems. Socio-economic problems of a country determine the aims of education. In India, we have a number of socio-economic problems. One of the objectives of education may be to establish a socialistic pattern of society which is in tune with the democratic setup of the country. Similarly, the educational system of the country is expected to produce socially and economically independent citizens who can contribute to the betterment of the country. In the words of Secondary Education Commission Report (1952-53): "As political, social and economic conditions change and new problems arise, it becomes necessary to re-examine and re-state clearly the objectives which education at each definite stage, should keep in view."

7. Exploration of Knowledge. Present age is the age of science and technology. There is almost an explosion of knowledge. Education today has become cosience-oriented and technology-based. It is thus evident that exploration of knowledge is an important factor in determining the aims of education.

Education must represent these factors and be related to the realities and problems of life.

HISTORICAL BACKGROUND

Aims of Education as history reveals, differed from time to time.

Here below are given the aims of education which were popularly advocated at different times:

Ancient India

1. To infuse in the learners piety and religiousness.
2. To form good character.
3. To inculcate civic and social duties.
4. To develop the personality fully.
5. To promote social efficiency and happiness.
6. To preserve and propagate culture.

Medieval India

1. Propagation of Islam.
2. Extension of Islamic kingdom.
3. Spread of education among Muslims.

4. Development of morality.
5. Building of character.
6. Achievement of material well-being.

British Rule

1. Consolidation of British Empire.
2. Recruitment of clerks.
3. Promoting craze for English articles and English textiles.
4. Spreading English Literature.
5. Preparing a class of interpreters of English laws.
6. Translating literary master pieces of Indian religious books into English.

Aims of Education are related to time and space. They are also changeable. The history of educational development in India stands evidence to this fact. There have been different aims of education in different periods. A brief account of aims of education in chronological sequence is given below:

Aims of Education in the Brahmanic Period. The aim of education during Brahmanic period was an all-sided development of man. Education was regarded as a means of salvation or emancipation. The chief aim of education was to unfold the spiritual and normal power of the individual. Education was thus determined by religious values.

The Aims of Buddhist Education. The aim of education during Buddhist period was to create a sense of equality among all, 'Satya' and 'Ahimsa' were the directive principles of this system of education. The child was taught to control and suppress his worldly desires in accordance with the eightfold code of conduct enunciated by Lord Buddha.

Aims of Education during Muslim Rule. The aim of education during the Muslim period was to prepare an individual for the wordly life as well as for the spiritual life. It was education of islamic culture and scriptures which regulated human behaviour accordingly.

Aims of Education during British Rule. The aims of education during British rule were different. The system of British education was implanted in this country with purely political motives. It aimed at dividing Indians spiritually and intellectually into the English-knowing class of men and non-English-knowing masses of people. It was in accordance with Macaulay's "Downward Filtration Theory."

New Social Trends

Aims of Education need careful fixation. They have to be in accordance with the needs and requirements of the individuals, the society, the nation and the situations prevailing all around. Aims of education have been different at different times. After the independence of the country Jawaharlal Nehru remarked, "Great changes have taken place in the country and the educational system must be keeping with them. The entire basis of education must be revolutionized." The society today is facing a number of problems. Social, political and economic conditions of the country are fast changing. It is, therefore, very important that we should assess everything carefully in the light of present situations and fix up aims of education which are suitable for the people of free India in every way. Suggested aims of education are:

1. Individual Aim of Education.
2. Social Aim of Education.
3. Vocational Aim of Education.
4. Character Building Aim.
5. Spiritual Aim of Education.

6. Harmonious Development Aim.
7. Cultural Aim of Education.
8. Knowledge Aim of Education.

Social and Individual Factors

Individual aim of education means that education should develop the individuals according to their interests and capabilities. It means free growth of individuality, helping every boy and girl to achieve the highest degree of individual development. Individuality is the ideal of life. An individual is the central figure in the social setup of life. All social institutions exist for the betterment and improvement of the individual. The individual is the end and these social institutions are the means. It is the fullest development of the individual. Education aims at training and development of the individual. It is only this type of individual who comes· out as a good citizen.

The individual aims of education have been emphasized by various thinkers. Their view points are as under:

The Naturalists like Rousseau believe that "The central aim of education is the autonomous development of the individual." According to him, "Everything is good as it comes from the hands of Author of Nature, but everything degenerates at the hands of man. God makes all things good. Man meddles with them and they become evil." This group of thinkers believe that man and citizen cannot be trained simultaneously. In short, education must secure those conditions where every individual is allowed to have a free play of his personality. He is free to develop his inherent, powers the highest potentialities of self.

The biologists believe that every individual is unique in his own way. G. Thompson believes that "Education is for the individual. Its function being to enable the individual to survive and live out its complete life. Education is imparted to preserve the individual life. Education is given for the sake of the individual to save him from destruction. Community exists for the individual, not the individual for the community. Community being the means and individual being the end, education should not set the means over the end." Therefore, individual and not society should be the centre of all educational efforts and activities.

According to the psychologists, education is an individual process. No two children are identical in intellectual capacity. Education must be individualized. Then only they can be benefitted fully.

The modern progressive thinkers also hold the view that the ultimate good of society lies in discovering the hidden value of the individual. In the words of Sir Percy Nunn, enters the human world except in end through the free activities of the individual men and women and that educational practice must be shaped to accord with the truth."

Each individual child should hold the key positions in the educative process. There is much force in the individual aim of education. However, individual aim, in its extreme form, is not desirable. The social aim has its own values and justification. This extreme and onesided view of individual aims has teen criticized.

The individual aim of education has been discussed on account of the following points:

Isolated Individual a Figment of Imagination. "An isolated individual" as, T. Rayment says, "is only a figment of imagination. We cannot conceive of an individual living and developing in isolation from society."

An Individual is a Social Being. In the words of John Dewey, "As a social being he is a citizen growing and thinking in a vast complex of interactions and relations." So an educational activity that does not swear by the social end, consequently fails even to serve the individual.

Individual must be Made Fit for Entire Society. Rusk says that the aim of education is not development of individuality but the enrichment of personality. Education must transform him from individual being to social being. He must be fit to live in the society.

The Basis of Individual's Greaters is Social. The contribution of great men (individual being?) when not isolated from the society. Their greatness was due to their assimilation of the rich Heritage of the society. They worked against some social background. Hence, the very basis of their great contributions was social.

In all, individual aim of education in its extra form is one sided. It is not in tune with the socio-political setup of the country. It may adversely affect the economy of the country as well. Those who believe in it are self-centred and perhaps selfish. It is all right to a limited extent. Society or state aim also very important.

A man in isolation is not considered good. He is known by the company he keeps or the society he belongs to. Surely the society or state is superior to the individual. That is my view-point of supporters of social aim of education.

In its extreme form, social aim regards individual only as a tool of society. He is subordinate to the society. Moreover, it cannot live without society.

Below are given the arguments of those who are in favour of social aim of education:

An Individual is an Integral Part of Entire Society. He is born in society and he grows and develops in society. Society should be given more importance as compared to the individual.

Education is under the Control State. State or society is to determine 'what' and 'how' of education. What should be taught to the individual and how it should be taught are determined by the society? Therefore, social aim is more important.

The Individual is Born with a Number of Raw Instincts. The society gives training to him. The good soft environment makes him a man. Social environment need be cared for more as compared to the individual.

Society Makes the Individual Civilized. It teaches him the lesson of citizenship. So the society or the social aims need be given more importance.

Security, Peace and Justice Exist in the Society. They are properly maintained in the society only. It is, therefore, urgently needed on the part of the individual that he should give importance to society.

Thus, we find that the social aim of education completely overpowers the individual.

Social aim of education in its extreme form has been criticized in many ways. It is certainly one-sided view. The following are the points of criticism:

1. It is unpsychological because it does not take into account the capacities and interests of the individual. Man becomes a means to an end. He has to sacrifice his own interests.

2. It ignores the needs, desires and interests of the individual and also suppresses his creative power.

3. It suppresses individual freedom, develops narrow nationalism and ignores the individual completely, it leaves no scope for the individual personality to flourish.

4. It tries to make the individual just a tool of the state. He forgets his own individuality and becomes a blind servant of the society.

5. The desires and aspirations of the individual are ended and he has to work for the good of the society. Thus education makes an individual a tool of the society. It may make the individual narrow-minded and in them there may develop all hatred for the society.

Are individual aims of education sufficient in themselves? Can we go on fully with their support? No, it is not possible. An individual cannot be thought of in a vaccum. Support of the society is a must for him. He is an integral part of the society. We shall have to think of betterment of society through the increase of education. Education is a very good weapon to cut off the itching sharpness of individual and social aims of education. They have certain drawbacks and those must be ended. Then the two—individual and soda! aims of education be synthesized. Surety, they are contemporary nature. Each one will become a support for the other. That way then, they will serve the purpose in far better ways.

Synthesizing the individual and social aims of education will create healthy and conducive environment which will ensure proper growth and development of the individual. There will be nothing bad for the individual no suppression of his creativeness. Better individual will give rise to a group of better individuals and that will naturally improve the society in every day.

Every individual has got the capacity to make the society grow and develop full. Everyone wants to see it prospering. For this achievement, the individual will have to be prepared for the self-sacrifice for the society. Education serves that purpose fruitfully. Education has two fold purpose: "The perfection of the individual and good of the community". Isolated individual is the figment of imagination.

An individual is like a plant and society is the soil or earth. No plant can grow in the absence of soil or earth. Social medium is needed for the proper growth of the individual. In the words of John Adam "individuality requires a social medium to grow, without social contacts we are not human." According to Ross, "individuality is of no value and personality is a meaningless term, apart from the social-environment in which they are developed and made manifest. Self-realization can be achieved only through social services and the social-ideas of real value can come into being only through free individuals who have developed valuable individuality. The circle cannot be broken."

There is no conflict between self-realization and social service as aim of life. It is, undoubtedly, right to say that the true aim of education is the highest development of the individual as a member of the society.

A few experts gave their views to favour it:

(i) Adams, "Self is realized in society through social interaction."

(ii) MacIver, "Socialization and individualisation are two sides of a single process."

(iii) In the words of Mahatma Gandhi, no conflict between individual and society. He says, "I believe that if one man gains spiritually, the whole world gains with him."

(iv) Nunn says, "individuality develops only in a social atmosphere where it can feed on common interests and common activities."

(v) According to Humayun Kabir: "If one is to be creative member of society, one must not sustain one's own

growth, but contributes something to the growth of society."

Thus we find that both the individual and the society are needed for making life full of fragrance and worthy of living. Initiative of the individual is important at its own place and social contact is needed to give the individual proper recognition and right-direction. Both supplement each other. So by synthesizing the two we shall be able to make the individual and the society grow and develop fully.

Professional Motives

Livelihood is important because without bread and butter, living is not possible. Edu :ation, therefore, must enable an individual to stand on his own feet and he should be able to earn for his living. Only a living person has certain needs and requirements. A dead person has no desire, no aspiration and no requirements. When we talk of a living person, we surely see to it from his all around point of view. An individual needs education in order to live. He needs education in order to live well. He needs education to do various things of life in a better way. They are possible with the help of money only. According to Secondary Education Commission, knowledge gained is useless if an individual cannot make both ends meet. Without a vocation, the individual is a drag and parasite on others. A social parasite cannot be called a free man. He begins to feel free only when he is economically independent. Vocational education, thus, exercises a liberalizing effect on man. There is no vocation without education. Every vocation has an educational value. Education with the vocational aim in the background will prepare each individual for an occupation. Vocational aim of education is also known as 'Bread and Butter aim', 'Blue Jacket Aim' and 'White Collar Aim.'

It has been rightly said that "Vocational Education is an education of most effective kind, for lack of which those who merely go to school, suffer all their lives." in the words of

Gandhiji, "True education ought to be a kind of insurance against unemployment."

Solves Economic Problems. Vocational aims make a person fit for some vocation. He becomes sound economically. In this age of material crisis, the problem of unemployment and underemployment are causing many economic problems. When education is vocation centred, it will help a lot.

Gives Social Status. Vocational aims bring vocational efficiency. With more money, a person feels satisfied in the society. It gives him good social status.

Suits to Average Learners. In every classroom, there are different types of learners. The good and brilliant are able to do well in studies. But the average types of learners find studies a big problem. Vocational education helps them, because it is suitable for them.

Helps in Moral Development. In the absence of vocation centred education, many students would become misfit for society. They will do every type of bad deeds to earn money for their living. Vocational education thus makes them morally good.

Makes a Person Active. In vocational education, the learners are able to develop their interests in the vocation. Quite a number of them are able to excel.

Makes Learning Useful. Vocational education makes learning useful. Here some vocation is of primary importance. The study of so-called traditional subjects is secondary.

A few experts pitt-forth their views as under:

Spens Report, "Preparation for vocation is an important part of our education."

Hartshorne's view, "Vocational education is an education of most effective kind, for lack of which those who merely go to school, suffer all their lives."

Demerits

1. Only vocational aim is not sufficient for an individual. Some studies are also needed. Social and cultural aims are in no way of lesser importance.

2. It is a narrow aim of education.

3. It is too much materialistic.

It we have a professionally good doctor or a professionally good engineer, it is not sufficient. There is need of a good man in each one of them. So just vocational aim is not sufficient. All other aims which make an individual a good person, are also fleeced.

Character is very important in the case of every learner, every teacher, every professional and above all, every person. In the absence of a good character, the whole personality stands zeroed. It is the soul of human body. Education for character is of top- most importance. It gives the man confidence and courage. A man of character is a man of word, is a true national, is a true citizen, and above all, a true human being. India needs today men of character. In them lie the hope and future prosperity of the nation. Only persons of character make the nation great and strong.

In the present day life, when there are erosion of higher values, education for character is the only way to solve the problems. Definitely the society of today is badly in need of higher values of life—Truth, Beauty and Goodness.

The chief aim of education should be 'character building.' Herbart summed up the concept of education as 'Morality.'

John Dewey says, "The establishing of character is a comprehensive aim of school instruction and discipline."

Swami Vivekanand says, "We want that education by which character is formed, strength of mind, is increased, the intellect is expanded and by which one can stand on one's own feet."

Raymont says, "The teacher's ultimate concern is to cultivate, not wealth or muscle, nor fulness of knowledge, nor refinement of feeling, but strength and purity of character."

'Gandhiji very dearly said, "Character building is the aim of education. I would try to develop courage, strength, virtue the ability to forget oneself in working towards great aims. I should feel that if we succeed in building the character of individual, society will take care of itself."

In the words Radhakrishannan, "The troubles of the whole world including India and the fact that education has become a mere intellectual exercise and not the acquisition of moral and spiritual values."

Personal Examples of Teachers and Administrators. The teachers and the administrators working in the schools should be living good examples of character. The learners come in contact with them every now and then and they observe them and watch them carefully at every moment. Only good teaching personnel will be able to imbibe the qualities of good character in the learners.

Moral Education as a Subject. Moral education as a subject should be introduced in the school curriculum. The different textbooks of all subjects of among or more education as a subject among me youths will naturally improve upon their moral behaviour. The earlier we start with this, the better it would be for the future of society and the nation.

Encourage the Students to Read Good Books. The teachers should recommend the study of good books to the students. Biographies of great men were really great in the true sense of the word should be purchased for the library. Such books should be within easy access of the students.

Then naturally the students will read those books "and learn lesson for all times to comes.

Projects for Honesty. A few projects for honesty may be started in the school. Students' Post Office, Students' Cooperative Store, Students' Canteen etc. may be started. The students should be given the charge of these activities under the guidance of some teacher and they should run it on 'No Profit, No Loss' basis. This will imbibe in the students qualities like sincerity, honesty and hard-work which will make them an asset for the society.

Celebration of Birth Days. The school should actually celebrate the birthdays of great religious leaders and saints. Instead of declaring a holiday on such days, celebration of the day highlighting the achievements and contributions of those great men will help the learners to learn many good things. Naturally it will improve upon their moral behaviour.

Lectures by Persons of High Moral Values. Some religious persons who are really saints of the society should be invited to the school for a lecture on moral education. Speech by them based on their studies and experiences of life will create interest in the students and also help them in becoming morally better students.

Merits

1. A person without character is like a man with body and without soul. So character building aim of education is really of primary importance.
2. Everybody needs be good human being. That is not possible without character. Therefore, character building as aim of education should be given top-most importance.

Demerits

1. Let there are not too much moral values. If we do so, other aspects of life stand neglected.

2. What is good and what is bad need to be known to everyone. Character aim is moral and that is for all. In its absence, it will be difficult to live well in a social group.

Education for culture is education to improve upon cultural aspect of the society. That improvement can be there only it we have the past and the present cultures available with us many good things we want to preserve, we want to refine and transmit in order to enrich our culture all the more. Cultural aspect of life is significant in its own way.

Cultural aim in narrow sense means dress, manners, way of life etc. In broader sense, it means good habits; good thoughts, etc. Surely cultural aim of education is grace to human life. Humanyun Kabir has rightly emphasized the importance of culture in the words: The continuity of culture and traditions is an essential condition for the survival of a nation. Culture is the foundation, the pifthary thing—it should snow itself in the smallest detail of your conduct and personal behaviour, how you sit, how you talk, how you dress, etc, inner culture must be reflected in your speech, the way in which you treat visitors and guests and behave towards one another and your teachers and elders.

Cultural Aspects

1. Ottaway said, "The culture of society means the total way of life of a society.
2. Methu Arnold said, "The best that has been thought and know is culture."
3. In the words of E.B. Taytor, "Culture is that complex whole which includes knowledge, belief art, moral law, custom and any other capabilities and habits acquired by man as a member of society."
4. Ellwood, "Culture includes on the one hand the whole of man's material civilization, tools, weapons,

systems of industry, and on the other, all the non-material or spiritual civilization such as language literature, art, morality, law and Government."

Merits

1. One comes to know about all the things then one can transmit or preserve them better.
2. A person culturally more sound is one who excels in one aspect, gains confidence and that helps to becoming better or other aspects of personality.
3. One can improve one's culture update it in the light of other cultures.
4. It adds grace to human. We, make it worth living as there is a keen desire to prosper, to flourish and to live-better and better.
5. One is able to understand society properly and can add to enrich' it and can also root out ills from it. One can also eliminate the bad elements from the culture.
6. It glorifies the nation, enriches its already rich cultural heritage.
7. It trains and cultivates human powers. John Dewey said that an individual is enabled to join freely and fully in shared or common activities.

Demerits

1. Too much emphasis on cultural aim will lead to neglect or other aspects of personality.
2. It hinders the natural development of the child. In the words of T.P. Nunn, "the aim of cultural-development-hinders a child from developing according to his own interests and potentialities."

He further says, "National institutions and traditions have a performance which made individual life a trivial thing."

3. It will be in line with the surrounding and the prevailing social climate.
4. A few bad things cannot be allowed to continue but in cultural aim that has to be continued. Long and fellow gap stated "Let the past bury its dead"
5. There are many cultures in the world which one is ideal and the best-it is difficult to decide, if we go on within our own culture, our vision may be narrow and may be too low.
6. It leads to neglect of professional aspect of education which is very important to earn one's livelihood.

Cultural aim of education is important but it cannot be given priority in the aims of education. It can surely assist the other aims with some broader thinking on it. In the words of Rafifidm, "India has to choose for herself a culture that derives inspiration from what is noble in our ancient culture and at the same time does not ignore demands of the present age."

Spiritual Aspects

Education makes a person spiritually sound. A person who is spiritually sound behaves better. He/she is able to do well while being trained for social efficiency, sound morality and physical betterment. In the absence of spiritual aim of education, one's life is incomplete. Spiritual aim is the pillar on which rests the edifice of total personality. Surely it is deeply linked with the character building aim. Spiritual aim gives strength to human soul and mind. The great spiritualists like Guru Nanak, Buddha, Mahavir, Swami Dayanand, Vivekanand, Shankaracharya, Aurobindo, Gandhiji, Tagore accepted the spiritual aim of education. Views of some of them on this aspect of life are given below and they are worth mentioning down:

> Aurobindo said, "Every man has in himself something divine, something his own, a chance of perfection and strength. In however small a sphere which God offers him to take or refuse. The task is to find it, develop it and use it. The chief aim of education should be to help the growing soul to draw out that in self which is best and make it perfect for a noble cause.
>
> Finfey said, "Material progress is good thing; social and political reforms are mere valuable both to the race and the individual; their final worth lies in the aid they afford to spiritual life."
>
> Dr. Radhakrishnan said, "The aim of education is neither national efficiency, nor world solidarity, but making the individual feel that he has within himself something deeper than intellect, call it spirit. If you like."

Merits

1. Spiritual aim of education makes a person gentle and pious.
2. It makes the students religious minded. They are able to have some values of life—and all this has its good effect on their behaviours.
3. It reduces the problems of indiscipline, conflicts, quarrels to some extent corruption, greed, aggression etc., destruction, hatred are on the increase. All these also stand checked to a considerable extent.
4. It makes the personality of the individual strong. He/she becomes a man of character, honesty and integrity.

Demerits

1. One may think of leaving the worldly life. That is not so good for everyone.
2. Spiritual aim may be achieved but one may not be so practical.

Spiritual aim of education, no doubt, is important but it cannot be given top-most priority in the aim of education. Other aims of education the vocational aim, knowledge aim, etc will to be cared for fully. Then and then and then only it will remain practical and useful to lead a good life in the society.

Harmonious development of personality is considered to be the main aim of education. In harmonious development, various facets of personality *i.e.,* academic, social, cultural, economic, spiritual, aesthetic etc. are fully cared for and they are given equal importance. Emphasis on all aspect of personality helps to have a balanced type of personality. In the process of education, different types of education are important in their own ways. Each one has great significance. None of them should be ignored considering it insignificant. One of them or two out of them should not be considered more important than others. Due recognition to each aim and that also on proportionate basis must be given. Then only there will be harmony in the various aspects of an individual's personality. A harmoniously developed individual is an asset not only to the social group or community but also to the society or the nation he belongs to. He is good, incarnate and he is bound to emit fragrance and imbibe in others goodness wherever he is and wherever he goes. Therefore, harmonious development aim of education is important and it must be properly attended to by one and all.

The great men say so about harmonious development aims Rousseau regards education as, "The process of development into an enjoyable, rational, harmoniously-balanced, useful and hence natural life."

In the words of Ross, "Harmonious development needs the intellectual, religious, moral and aesthetic development of the child."

Pestalozzi says, "Education is natural, harmonious and progressive development of man's innate powers." By harmonious development, he means the education of head, heart and hand.

In this context Gandhiji said, "By education I mean an all round drawing out of the best in child and man—body, mind and spirit," He further says, "Man is neither mere intellect, nor the gross animal, nor the heart and soul alone. A proper and harmonious combination of all the three is required for the making of the whole man and constitutes the true economics of education."

Merits

1. An individual comes out all round good. He is successful in whatever type of situation he is placed.
2. He is academically good, physically and mentally sound, normally and culturally all rights has social efficiency and is economically a fit person for some vocation.

Demerits

1. Development of all aspects is not possible fully in one way or the other, one may lag behind.
2. It is not possible to measure accurately whether the desired ends are reached or not.
3. Harmonious development aim is good within this age of competitions where only academic aspect is

the main criteria, the person may not get a chance of selection.

4. Individual differences are always there.

5. The problems of population explosion, unemployment hinder the harmonious development of the individual.

6. In some institutions, all facilities for harmonious development of personality are not available. Moreover, it is very difficult to decide a suitable curriculum for it.

Academic Aspects

Knowledge is very important these days. A person with good and up-to-date knowledge is able to impress others. Such a person gets applaud whatever he is and wherever he goes. Education equips a person with adequate knowledge. It updates his knowldge aim of education. Is it the most important aim of education? The answer to this has to be thought of carefully. Knowledge is not the only thing important in life. An individual stands adorned with knowledge. Apart from academic aspect, other aspects of personality *i.e.*, physical aspect, social, cultural, moral, educational are in no way of lesser importance. One thing is definite that knowledge about social, cultural, moral aspects is possible only if

Merits

The following are the merits of knowledge aim of education:

1. It is a very good instrument of education.

2. It helps the individual as well as the society in the proper growth and development.

3. It helps the individual in making adjustment in life.

4. It strengthens morality.
5. It makes an individual thoughtful.

Demerits

1. Knowledge for the sake of knowledge is not good.
2. More knowledge is good but it is add out the cost of starving the soul.

Aims of education must be related to the needs and requirements of the people. In this fast changing age when values of life are changing, life is becoming complex and to live well is a challenge for everyone. Education should equip a person to face life boldly and courageously, eradicate its shortcomings and make it worthy of living. Education must enable an individual to come out all successful in every walk of life whatever may be the situation—political, social, cultural and whatever may be the circumstances of the individual. Then and then only education will be called education worth the name—an instrument of utility and usefulness for humanity.

The Commission made a bold statement in respect of aims of education for democratic India. It stated that education must develop in its citizens habits, attitudes, and qualities of character and equip them to bear the burden of life in the changing economic structure. The Commission suggested the following aims of education:

Development of Democratic Citizenship. It is the major responsibility of education to carefully train every citizen for democratic citizenship. Such a training comprises of:

Receptive to New Ideas. The individual becomes open minded. He welcomes new ideas at every stage. He is not a narrow thinking individual tied to the old customs and traditions. He is always willing to accept the change.

Clear Thinking. Education should equip the individual with the capacity of clear thinking. The individual should be a good democratic citizen who is clear of head and clear at heart. This makes him have clear thinking about everything.

Clearness in Speech and Writing. The individual has clarity in speech and in writing. While exchanging ideas with others orally, he remains peaceful. While writing maintains clarity and is able to present ideas with full clarity.

Art of Living with the Community. The individual learns to live with others. He believes in cooperation and co-existence. He is a social being ever-ready to learn the art of living with community.

True Patriotism. The individual is a true patriot through and through. He leaves narrow ideology of selfishness in the interest of broaded national feelings. He is well-wisher of a nation and whatever he does or says, he remains in tune with the nation.

Development of Internationalism. Education imbibes the qualities of world citizenship. He believes in universal brotherhood. Today, just patriotism is not sufficient. There is need of true and pure nationalism which believes in internationalism.

Improvement of Vocational Efficiency. Education must aimed at increasing the productive or vocational efficiency of young students. It includes:

(a) Realization of the national prosperity is possible only through work.

(b) A new attitude toward work and dignity of labour.

The emphasis should be on crafts and productive work and diversification of courses. The ideas is that a large number of students may take up vocational courses.

Development of Personality. Education should develop hence, artistic and cultural interests of the students. These are necessary for self-expression and for the full development of human personality. For this purpose subjects like art, craft, music, dancing etc should be included in the scheme of studies.

Education for Leadership. In order make democracy function successfully, it is essential 'To' incutctr—the qualities of leadership in youth. Education should train the youth to provide leadership in the social, poflfical, industrial and Itural fields.

Indian Education Commission (1964-66) has made very valuable recommendation regarding the aims of education. It has, in fact, turned to refer to the whote system of education through its recommendations, the Commission has stated, "No reform is more urgent than to transform education, endeavour to relate it to the life, and thereby make it a powerful instalment of social, economic and cultural transformation, necessary for the realization of our-national goals."

The Commission is suggested the following aims of education for the purpose of reforming it:

1. Increasing Productivity.
2. Promoting Social and National integration.
3. Accelerating the process of Modernization.
4. Cultivating social, moral and spiritual values.

The details of these aims are given below:

Increasing Productivity. It is very essential to increase the productivity of a country in order to ensure its progress. This objective can be achieved by education. The commission has suggested to act upon the following programmes in order to achieve this goal.

Indian Education Commission described the promotion of social and national integration as the main objective of education because the unity of the nation is the only solid basis of the strength of a country. The Commission recommended the following steps to be taken for this purpose:

Common Schools. There should be common schools for all students, belonging to any category or community.

There is a great need of continuous progress in the country so that we should be able to walk side by side with other countries of the world. Hence, there is an urgent need of accelerating the process of modernization in our country so that we may be able to stand in line with the developed countries of the world. For this purpose, there is a great need for the use of science based on technical education. There is also a need for preserving and re-evaluating the cultural heritage of our country so that we may be able to move forward in every field of life.

The commission has given the following suggestions for this purpose:

(i) Education should create the feeling of curiosity and investigation through the development of proper interests, sentiments and attitudes. There is also a need for developing the power of dear thinking and decision-making in the students.

(ii) Education should create perfect intelligentsia which should be associated with the different categories of people and which should have deep roots in the soil of the country.

Indian Education Commission had laid great emphasis on cultivating social, moral and spiritual values In order to associate education with Indian Culture Religious or moral education has always enjoyed a great importance in India. Everyone in this country wants that education should cultivate good qualities, moral values and spiritual understanding among the students so that they may cultivate these good qualities in other persons. The Commission has given the following suggestions in this connection.

(i) There should be an arrangement in the school time table for teaching fundamental principles of all religions.

(ii) The knowledge of becoming a good citizen should be made a part of education.

(iii) Social, moral, religious and spiritual qualities should be developed in students through practical working in the school.

The Assessment

We should try to make a critical evaluation of the present system of education in the light of the aims of education suggested by the Indian Education Commission. The critical evaluation reveals to us the following things:

1. The present system of education has proved itself to be quite unsuccessful in creating good citizens. The standard of citizenship is falling day by day in our country because of the spread of corruption and indiscipline. And in general, there is fall in moral values.

2. Unsuccessful in Creating all Round Development. The present system of education in our country is quite unsuccessful in creating all round development in students. Our education lays great stress on intellectual development only. It ignores physical, economic, social and cultural development of the students.

3. Vocational education is not being given in the planned way in our country. No doubt, vocational education

has been started in some schools, but the students are not given proper guidance in the selection of suitable vocations. They are not given any information of the opportunities of employment in various vocations.

4. No religious education is given to the students in our schools. As a result of it love for all religions has disappeared in our country and fanaticism has become the order of the day.

5. Our education has also been unsuccessful in cultivating moral values in the students. As a result of it, moral standard of people is falling day-by-day many persons in the country have become selfish and greedy.

6. Our education has proved itself to be unsuccessful in developing national unity. Our teachers and education have not been able to convey the concept of national unity to the students. Nothing has been done to establish common schools in India as suggested by Indian Education Commission. The students belonging to various religions are not given opportunities to work together freely. Hence our students have not understood and developed the concept of national unity.

Following are the ideal aims of education at the present time:

1. All round or perfect development of the personality of all the students.
2. Preparing students for the service of humanity.
3. Creating good citizens out of all the students.
4. Imbibing the spirit of patriotism in the students.

5. Cultivating the spirit of social and national unity in the minds of students.

6. Enabling the students to preserve their cultural heritage.

7. Making proper use of Human Resources.

8. Imparting vocational education for enabling the students to earn their livelihood.

9. Giving moral, religious and spiritual education to students in order to raise their moral, and ethical standards.

10. Creating awareness in the minds of the students for modernization.

❋❋❋

3

Features and Principles of Educational Administration

Dr. E.A. Pires calls that system of educational administration good in which there are evidences of democratic leadership in the implementation of educational policies democratically determined. Educational administration at any level should be a cooperative and democratic process. A good administrator would do well if he uses 'we' and not 'I' in emphasising the achievements of the department or of institution. This gives a sense of pride to his colleagues and they think that due regard is given to their merits.

Significant Features

Bossing suggests six characteristics of the leadership needed in the high school principalship:

1. Ability to Inspire. The principal must be a leader and not an automation or a despot. One crucial test of the principal's competency must be his ability to inspire and lead teachers, not drive them.

2. Imagination. Imagination must be a second requisite of the leader of the secondary school.

3. Educational Expert. Contrary to the emphasis of the past the leader of our democracy's school must be first and foremost an educational expert and secondarily a master of administrative technique the principal is above all else an educational leader who must understand the nature of education and the educational process and give leadership to the educational problems of the school and the community.

4. Man of Contact. To render effective leadership in school and community the principal must be much more than a pusher of buttons. The principal should be a man of wealth of contacts, direct and vicarious.

5. Social and Educational Philosophy. Finally, but not least in importance, the leadership for the secondary school of today must possess a well defined social and educational philosophy. He must have a clear understanding of the basic philosophies of life and values upon which different contemporary societies are based. He should understand the basic difference between the philosophy of fascism and that of democracy. The place and importance of the school in our democratic society and the relationship of such of its parts in the creation of intelligent democratic citizens he must fully appreciate.

6. Adventurous Spirit. All this requires a leader for the secondary school who possesses an unflagging adventurous spirit and an experimental attitude toward his problems.

Head and Subordinates

Delicate and Critical Role of the Principal. The principal has to play a very delicate and critical role as he has to strike a balance in the practical field among fighting and quarrelling students, grudging and grumbling teachers and complaining parents. The members of the teaching staff have their different whims: some sensitive, some emotional, some enthusiastic, some old, some young, some trained and other untrained and some marking time. The principal has to make the best use of them and seek their whole-hearted cooperation in all the activities of the school: academic, cocurricular and administrative.

"Encouragement in one case, assistance in overcoming difficulties in another, suggestions here, definite orders there, all are necessary," writes R.G. Stead. The principal has to weld the members of the staff into a real team.

The Principal is expected at various times and by various interests to play many roles. He must by nature of his position be:

(a) A Teacher of teachers.

(b) A Disciplinarian just but effective.

(c) A Supervisor not only of teachers but of service personnel.

(d) A Psychologist at least to the extent of discovering maladjustments, especially of teachers which hinder progress.

(e) A Lawyer to the extent of being able to know his own obligations, rights, legal abilities as well as of those of all school personnel.

(f) A Sociologist to the extent of understanding the relationships of the school with social forces.

(g) A Financier in organizing the school budget.

(h) A Technical Expert in educational measurement and evaluation.

(i) An Expert in Group Dynamics to the extent of working effectively with staff, pupils, public and the authorities.

Basic Principles

Principle of Democratic Administration. We have already discussed that a Head should follow the principles of democratic administration. According to K.G. Saiyidain, "To my mind a good Headmaster is one who can inspire and enthuse his colleagues without dominating over them like a hard task master."

Principle of Sharing Responsibility. He should be prepared to share the control and authority with his colleagues. He should not think that he is born to rule and should not desire to be on the top of everything in the school, *i.e.,* the president of games, the chairman of literary societies and the patron of social service and health unions, etc. The different departments should be placed under the charge of the senior members of the staff. Principle of 'Sharing Responsibility' should be the keynote of his policy. Supervision of the examinations, school cleanliness, morning assembly, funds, hostel, scouting, literary and social activities are some of the chief duties which would be delegated by the Headmaster to the other members of the staff.

Principle of Mutual Consultation. The Headmaster should frequently consult his colleagues regarding improvement in school discipline and instruction. Such consultations instil in them the spirit that they belong to the school and are as responsible to it as the Headmaster is. Staff meetings should be called from time to time. The teachers should be given full freedom to put forth their problems in these meetings. Briggs found that the teachers expected in a staff meeting *(i)* help on their problems, *(ii)* the wider outlook in education, *(iii)* meeting to be happy and wholesome, *(iv)* meeting based on appreciation of effort and accomplishment rather than shortcomings and faults. The head of the institution should take note of the teachers' problems and accordingly give his suggestions for the solution of the problems concerned.

Principle of Constructive Criticism. The criticism offered by the Headmaster should be judicious, fair and constructive rather than destructive. Supervision should be a matter of inspiration to teachers. It should be moderate. Excessive supervision kills all the initiative and drive of teachers. The role of a policeman or a military officer does more harm than good.

Principle of Human Relationships. A good Headmaster keeps in view the humane factor while dealing with the members of the staff. He treats them just like friends and does not say anything to them in the presence of the students and their parents which may lower their prestige. He does not give them suggestions regarding methods of teaching when they are taking their classes but gives the same by calling them in his office and tries to avoid all 'bossing tendencies'. The teacher should come out of the Headmaster's office a better person, wiser and in a more pleasant mood than he was when he went in his office. Autocratic heads are always ready to snub any pupil or teacher who puts questions to them and are easily annoyed when their colleagues differ from them.

Principle of Friendly Supervision. Speaking about administrators of tomorrow D.I. Lal observes, "He gives up the time-old tradition of checking his teachers, frightening his teachers, weakening his teachers and examining them, but manipulates things so as to train his teachers, inspire his teachers and trust them. In this way he will not only create an excellent professional moral among the teaching staff but will also cultivate a vital interest in them for educational philosophy, so that they can continually test and re-test their plans and purposes, ideas, ideals, methods and procedures, systems and organizations."

Principle of Cooperation. On the close cooperation of the Headmaster and the staff depends on the efficiency of the school arid the head of the institution is to a great extent responsible for securing cooperation of teachers. According to Reavis, "No matter what his personal characteristics are, he will not be successful unless he is able to inspire his associates and collaborators with the desire to work cooperatively for the goals for which the school stands. He will be judged by his ability to enlist and to utilize their ability in participating in the solution of school problems and in formulating educational policies that have the common objective of advancing the welfare of the children enrolled in the school. He does not attempt to conceal that he is their leader, but he does not on the other hand remind them what he is."

Jacobson observes, "The Principal should not interrupt classes, create disturbances on entering and leaving, or to take the class away from the teacher, unless invited to do so. If the Principal stays to the end of the class period he should observe good manners by expressing in a sentence or two his pleasure in visiting the class but refrain from making condemnatory statements until there is sufficient time to discuss them at length, if indeed he indulges in them at all."

1. Take the first step in being friendly.
2. Be cheerful.
3. Be easily accessible to the staff.
4. Be polite and courteous.
5. Remember and use names.
6. Take interest in the out of school activities of the members of the staff.
7. Take prompt action on requests.
8. Avoid taking special privileges.
9. Avoid keeping people waiting.
10. Keep a record of promises and live up to them.
11. Let people know when their work is good.

12. Be willing to listen.
13. Be concerned about the way a teacher feels about his job and his out of school life.
14. Ask persons if they are willing to assume responsibility.
15. Give praise for reporting facts accurately.
16. Avoid giving advice.
17. Offer services to assist in seeking agreement when disagreements arise in the group.
18. Visit teachers who are ill.
19. Become fully informed about the social structure of the staff.
20. Refuse to accept the assumption that conflicting groups in staff are unavoidable.
21. Keep in mind while preparing your schedule that other teachers are not put to inconvenience.
22. Give teachers a chance to tell their side of the story.
23. Show consideration for bashful teachers.
24. Attempt to see actions and decisions from the other persons point of view.
25. Give credit to the persons responsible when the school receives praise.
26. Do not make personal remarks to shame them.
27. Do not embarrass a teacher of inferior ability or one who has physical defects.
28. Show consideration for the feeling of other teachers.
29. Be willing to help teachers secure better positions.

30. Find out how different teachers wished to be treated and treat them accordingly.
31. Make changes slowly, preferably at teachers' suggestions.
32. Learn to work, to play, to live successfully with your associates.
33. Do not laugh at the actions which seem funny to you.
34. Learn to like people.
35. Avoid any evidence of authority.
36. Smile! As they say in the Navy, "a happy ship is a good ship" so, too, a happy school is a good school.
37. Criticize only in private.
38. Ask questions that relieve anxiety about discussing a problem.
39. Seek the help of teachers as co-workers and special advisers.
40. Always ask a teacher's permission to break into a classroom activity.
41. Be sincerely interested in teachers, like them as persons. Lincoln said, "If you wish to win a man to your cause, first convince him that you are his sincere friend."
42. Inform new teachers on matters of school regulation.
43. Do not show any undue favour to any member of the staff.
44. Give teachers your undivided attention both when listening and when talking to them.

45. Help teachers in difficulty with pupils, parents or other teachers.

Gathering of the Staff

Efficient running of the school demands that members of the staff should occasionally meet for sharing responsibilities as well as experiences. These meetings should be presided over by the Principal. These may be convened from time to time.

Briggs found that teachers expected the following things in a staff:

(i) Help in their problems.

(ii) Meeting to be happy and wholesome.

(iii) A wider outlook on education.

(iv) Meeting based on appreciation of effort and accomplishment rather than shortcomings and faults.

Planning of Staff Meetings. The teachers should be informed in advance of the problems to be discussed in the meetings. It is very important for the head to listen to every teacher with attention and care. Minutes of staff meetings should be kept if possible. A limit must be put to staff meetings and the best appears to be once a month. Of course, there need not be any rigidity in observing this principle. Occasional meetings for some particular purposes may have to be called. Sometimes it may become necessary for the head to convey staff meeting to clarify certain points of written order issued by him. An atmosphere of cheerfulness should prevail in all such meetings.

The head of the institution should take note of the teachers' problems and accordingly give his suggestions for the solution of the problems concerned. His attempt should be to help the teachers as much as possible. Time of meeting should be such as most of the members of the staff find it convenient to attend. Staff meetings should not be too long. Usually not more than one and a half hours be spent upon these.

Characteristics of Staff Meetings

1. All discussions should be above the personal level.
2. Discussion should not go off the track.
3. They should start in time.
4. They should be economical in time.
5. They should result in concrete suggestions.

The formation of Staff Club will facilitate intimate contacts between the head and the members of the staff and also among the members of the staff themselves. One member of the staff should serve as a secretary who should be elected every year so that most of the members get a chance of leading others.

The functions of the club would be recreational-cum-educational. It may arrange tea during recess for the staff members. Its another function would be to arrange welcome and farewell parties. Its third function will be to arrange excursions and picnics on holidays. Its fourth function will be to arrange discussions on important school problems.

The Head should not look upon this club with suspicion. He should occasionally attend meetings of the club. Through such informal meetings, he will learn more about the members of the staff and this will also help in cementing the bonds of friendship, goodwill and mutual understanding.

Relationship with Students

Often it is seen that the Headmaster makes the error of not coming into direct contact with the students. He should not forget that he can directly influence them to a considerable extent and as such he must avail himself of every opportunity of addressing them and attending various functions organized in the school. Regarding his work and relations with the students, we may quote Dr. V. S. Jha : "A good Headmaster or Principal is not merely a scholar, he is a man of sound character, deep sympathy and understanding and considerable tact and experience dealing with pupils. He should be profoundly sensitive to the physical, mental, moral and spiritual needs of the pupils and should know how to minister them."

The Headmaster must view the educational programme as a whole and assist students directly in having a balanced experience in terms of individual needs. To accomplish this he should:

- Show by action and in discussion that he places values in educational objectives over and beyond academic achievement: positive attitudes, citizenship skills, aesthetic appreciation, individual initiative, cooperative tendencies, etc.
- Give leadership to planning student activities, clubs and projects which will supplement and complement the academic class work.
- Make it a practice to get to know students personally, showing friendship to them and expressing interest in what they are doing.
- Approach individual student's problems from a guidance point of view, and help teachers to recognize individual differences in teaching and in dealing with students' problems.
- Involve students in real responsibility for the operation of significant aspects of the school, through student government, the house system and other techniques.

Relationship with Parents

Educators and administrators are now fast realizing that effective and intimate relations with parents are very necessary for the efficient organization of school work and activities. The head of an institution must find out ways and means for establishing happy contacts with student's parents and guardians.

His treatment with the parents should be very courteous. As Ryburn puts it, "He should always treat parents with scrupulous courtesy when they come to the school."

Schools serving the public in a democracy should be responsive to the wishes of parents regarding the school programme. Also, the school programme should be related to the community. Towards these ends the Headmaster should:

- Encourage parents to make constructive suggestions on ways of improving the school, providing avenues through which parents' ideas are reported and discussed.
- Assist the school staff in knowing the community and in teaching students ways in which they can contribute to community development.
- Arrange a variety of means for keeping the public informed about the school programme; new projects, progress in achieving objectives, and problems should be reported regularly.
- Make the school facilities available for use by appropriate community groups for meetings, recreation and adult education.
- Organize ways in which parents and community groups can help the school, through fund raising for specific activities, making community educational resources more readily available to the school, and

assisting teachers and students in studying the community.

Principal's Merits

Hundreds and thousands of eyes watch him, judge him, measure him and are eager to follow his noble example.

He has to be sweet and soft as well as stiff and stem.

Unless he has a seeing eye; an understanding heart and an all adjusting mental poise, he is bound to falter and tumble.

He should be firm in his dealings, resolute in his conviction and decisions, relentless in their execution.

Academically and Professionally Well-equipped. He must familiarize himself with the methods of teaching different subjects. Through the study of educational journals and periodicals and latest literature, he should keep himself well-posted regarding the latest developments in the field of education. He reads a lot and travels a lot.

(i) Possesses extensive knowledge of a school subject of his choice.

(ii) Possesses extensive knowledge in the field of education.

(iii) Applies scientific methods in dealing with problems.

(iv) Possesses extensive knowledge in broad areas of fields and experiences other than education.

(v) Respects men of scholarship.

(vi) Encourages through scholarship rather than superficiality.

Aware of What a Good Organization is. To quote J.B. Sears, an ideal head recognizes that, "a good organization is an arrangement of persons wherein its members may work effectively, economically and harmoniously together to achieve a common purpose, an arrangement of persons, which, as far as possible, may guard effectively against interference with its purposes and processes, an arrangement of persons which relies as much upon the common will, the initiative and the understanding of its members as it does upon authority, to energize or guide it and that applies to the concepts, also in its relations with those whom it serves."

Capacity to Make Favourable Impression Upon Others. An ideal Headmaster is able to make favourable impression upon all those who come in contact with him. His words, manners and behaviour win confidence of others. His talk is cultured, behaviour dignified, manners affable, conversation engaging, disposition amiable, imagination enlightened and attitude flexible.

Sultan Mohi-ud-din states, "Dignity does not consist in aloofness and in maintaining air of superiority; it rather consists in being helpful and doing the right thing. Great Headmasters have always been great friends of their pupils."

Considers on Aspect of his Work as Trivial. The same writer further writes, "Since he ceaselessly strives to be a model to others, he regards no aspect of his work as trivial or insignificant which can conveniently be passed on to others to be done well or ill." He is too well aware of the truth of that wise statement, "Trifles make perfection and perfection is no trifle." Hence every item be it the folding of a sheet or the writing of a circular—is done with meticulous care as if it were a religious act.

Considers the Administrative Machinery as all Instrument of Social Service. "An educational administrator is more than an official punctilious about administrative routine, he is a leader guiding and directing a sacred undertaking. The official apparatus that is at his disposal, the education department that is under his control, is more than a bureaucratic machine. It is an instrument of social service."

—Chitra Naik

Cooperative Attitude. "The leader of the school can be successful only when he secures willing cooperation from his coworkers; when he makes those co-workers feel that the problems of the school are theirs and not his own."

—Mohi-ud-din

Democratic Attitude. "A democratic administrator should look upon the personnel as socially equal to himself, he should not take decisions by himself, but with his colleagues, he should make them feel responsible and share in administration, he should have a code of set rules of administration which he and his colleagues should follow rigidly, making no discrimination in their application, and lastly, he should have no special privilege." **—R.R. Kumria**

Expert in Human Relations. An ideal head always remembers that all people cannot be equally intelligent and hard working. A trouble shooter needs to be handled firmly in the very beginning. Praise and appreciation sometimes help even if a person does not deserve it. Sometimes sympathetic hearing is all that is needed to blow off the steam of emotions. Sometimes valuable suggestions help in easing the tension.

Firm Attitude. He should be firm in his dealings, resolute in his conviction and decisions, relentless in their execution.

Faith in Human Nature. "It is essential, therefore, that he be a man of faith, faith in his vocation, faith in his pupils, faith in human nature and faith in himself."

Friend of the Students. The great Headmasters have always been great friends of their students. The Headmaster should possess the following skills:

1. Shows friendliness towards individual students.
2. Shows a spirit of 'oneness' and 'belongingness' with them.
3. Loves them intensely.
4. Shows interest in student activities.
5. Takes a keen interest in the welfare of the students.
6. Spares time for conferences.
7. Shows due regard to their personality.
8. Gives due regard to student opinion.
9. Shows a keen interest in solving their problems.

Gives Recognition to Good Work Done. Ryburn writes, "Nothing will more encourage a man or woman, a boy or a girl, to greater effort than an encouraging recognition of good work done, of sincere effort made, or good qualities shown. If those in charge of institutions and those carrying on the administrative work of departments wish to enable those working with them to do their best, they should always realize the value of ungrudging recognition of all that merits recognition."

Good at Office Correspondence. Office work is becoming a very taxing job day-by-day for the headmaster. Filing work should be maintained systematically and scientifically so that promptness is achieved in correspondence.

1. Gives judgement only after weighing and considering relevant evidence.
2. Decides cases promptly.
3. Decides cases on the basis of principles rather than expediency.
4. Perceives true qualities of people.

Health. "A person with indifferent health and poor stamina will not be able to discharge his own or discharge the multifarious and heavy responsibilities of his office."

—**Jaswant Singh**

Leader by Courage and Reason and not by Power. "He must learn to lead by reason, by his larger knowledge and courageous enthusiasm rather than to drive by reason of his superior power. He must reach up out of the routine of school supervision and execute duties into the higher level of educational statesman." —**E.P. Cubberly**

His Life is One of Immolation. In the words of S. Balakrishna Joshi, "The progress of the school community is his thought by day and dream by night, and his aching passion is to wear himself out in the service of the shrine in which he feels spiritually wedded. It is his conviction that while the life of a teacher is one of consecration that of the Headmaster should be one of immolation."

Man of Integrity. He fights all temptations to pad his purse with money to which he is not entitled. To quote S. Balakrishna Joshi, "He does not try to exploit school influence for private gains because he realizes that if he does it, he signs his moral death warrant. The result is that no amount of pressure can wean him from the path of duty and justice. Authority cannot coerce him, nor can temptation reduce him into any course of conduct, nor conducive to the highest interests of the school."

Optimistic Outlook. He has unlimited faith in himself. He does not accept defeat. He always thinks of success all the time. Ryburn stresses, "It is essential, therefore, that he be not only a man of high character but also that he be a man of faith; faith in his vocation, faith in his students, faith in human nature, and faith in his staff. "

"Go slow the first day, the first week, the first month, and even the first year, make changes slowly and always with the cooperation of the faculty," **—William T. Melchor**

Planning Capacity. "If a Principal is not careful, he will find himself spending much of the time in answering telephone, running errands for teachers, signing excuses, making repairs to the buildings, handling money, raising campaigns, and performing other minor duties and then budget his time accordingly." **—Margaret Grag**

Progressive Outlook. "It is reasonable to expect that a Head master should be progressive in his outlook." **—Mohi-ud-din**

Recognition for Good Work Done. "Nothing will more encourage a man or woman, a boy or a girl, to greater effort, than an encouraging recognition of good work done, of sincere effort made, or good qualities shown. If those in charge of institutions and those carrying on the administrative work of departments wish to enable those working with them to do their best, they should always realize the value of ungrudging recognition of all that merits such recognition." **—Ryburn**

Rises Equal to Any Occasion. "He rises equal to any occasion, and by his resourcefulness and readiness to render service, solves knotty problems. To him it is not beneath his dignity to strike the gong in time if the peon is engaged otherwise, or to lead a band of devoted volunteers to flush the latrines if scavenger is absent. Again he is prepared to 'referee' a match if the umpire has not turned up or step into a class and teach any subject if a teacher is called suddenly. Thus his willingness and ability to do any piece of work pertaining to the school, wrest for him the confidence and regard of all concerned."

Scientific Attitude. An ideal head is particularly careful in making judgement about persons for whom he cherishes a positive like or dislike. He observes correctly without letting personal feelings, prejudices, and wishes to influence him, draws valid conclusions from given facts and makes sound generalizations as the facts warrant. He does not see things through coloured spectacles. He is able to detach his personal likes and dislikes from the performance of others. He is conscious of the fact that monopoly of truth is not held by anyone.

Sense of Humour. Dr. Jaswant Singh writes about this quality, "It will enable him to get over an impasse with the help of a smile, a light hearted chuckle, or a jocular remark which will ease the tense atmosphere. The sense of humour will help break resistance, overcome opposition by injecting a spirit of camaraderie into the situation. Many a difficult situation can be resolved by a witty remark."

Sensitive to the Needs of the Students. "A good Headmaster should be profoundly sensitive to the physical, mental, moral, intellectual and spiritual needs of his pupils and should know how to minister to them." **—V. S. Jha**

Sensitive to the Many Sided Development of the Child. According to Dr. V. S. Jha, "He should be profoundly sensitive to the physical, mental, moral, intellectual and spiritual needs of the pupils and should know how to minister to them."

Thinking Capacity. "Experience is an indispensable qualification for a headmaster. This is certainly true. But experience alone without the capacity to think out and plan out new progressive programmes is inadequate."

—Mohi-ud-din

Vision and Imagination

1. Makes decisions which later events show to be sound and reliable.

2. Searches new practices and techniques.
3. Seizes opportunities to develop new patterns of action.

Qualities of the Headmaster

To justify his place as the inspiring leader and guide, the Head master must have a strong personality. R.A. Lamb remarks. "To make the perfect head of the school, there is needed in addition to all these, a quality which is undefinable—and which resides in the personality of the individuality. It is not possible to analyze this quality any more than it is possible by dissecting a man's brain to find wherein resides the soul or the spirit of life. But that it exists is beyond question."

Significance of the each letter of the word "Headmaster"

H stands for

(i) Hard work *(ii)* Helpfulness *(iii)* Honesty *(iv)* Humility *(v)* Humorous nature

E stands for

(i) Enthusiasm *(ii)* Ethics of the teaching profession *(iii)* Experimental attitude

A stands for

(i) Accuracy *(ii)* Adaptability *(iii)* Alertness *(iv)* Amicability *(v)* Attentiveness *(vi)* Attractive manner

D stands for

(i) Definiteness of aim *(ii)* Dependability *(iii)* Desire for self-improvement *(iv)* Devotion to the democratic ideal *(v)* Devotion to the profession

M stands for

(i) Mastery of the subject matter *(ii)* Mental development

S stands for

(i) Self-discipline *(ii)* Self-reliance *(iii)* Sincerity *(iv)* Sociability

T stands for

(i) Tact *(ii)* Truthfulness *(iii)* Teaching skill *(iv)* Training

R stands for

(i) Reasoning *(ii)* Resourcefulness *(iii)* Relationships.

Need for Raising the Status of Headmasters

The Education Commission felt, "It is also essential to give wider powers to Headmasters and greater freedom to schools. At present, the Headmasters as a class have been neglected. It will be seen that in our proposals, better scales of pay have been recommended... The general principle should be ... to vest them with necessary authority. They might commit mistakes—as all human beings do. But unless the freedom to commit mistakes is given, no headmaster will be able to take deep interest in the school and in its improvement."

4

Organization Models

In general, one subject is a model for something else when the concepts of both subjects are isomorphic. This means that there is a one-to-one correspondence between the concepts and assumptions of the model and the observed world, and the relationships take the same form. Isomorphism suggests hypotheses. For example, if a school system is like the human body, then the main office of the system may function like a brain, and decision processes may be likened to a nerve centre. Since a disturbance in one part of the body affects all other parts, the same may be expected of the school system. However, some of the disadvantages of models school also be apparent in the same illustration, because models are seldom perfect analogies, they can be seriously misleading. Yet sometimes they are used to the point of seeming real, they may become so sacred that the investigator is more interested in pre-serving the model than in interpreting reality. Because of such disadvantages, a model may actually obscure the actual relationships. This is especially true when models are chosen on the basis of their prestige or their success in other fields rather than any isomorphism or inherent similarities to the subject matter being studied. The prestige of physical science models may be a consideration that underlies their prevalence in the social sciences. For social science he relied heavily on physical, geological, and ecological models, and none of them are particularly relevant to social conduct. Models derived from cultural activities, such as the dramaturgical or even the musical model, have been ignored despite their possible relevance to everyday life.

Rational Models

Models in which conflict is the basic process are implicit throughout this book, but, since the biological models stressing structure have been among the most popular sociological models, the conflict models will be contrasted with them. Rational-biological models of organization in particular have widespread popularity among the most eminent contemporary theorists of organization, including C. I. Barnard and Talcott Parsons.

Gouldner describes the rational model as that model in which organization is conceived as a means for the realisation of announced group goals. Stress is placed on rationally directed, long-range development of the organization, or a system, toward explicitly stated goals. The model, as Gouldner points out, has called attention to the most distinguished characteristic of modern organization, its rationality. Its premises are that decisions are based on a rational survey of the situation and implemented through a codified legal apparatus, and that significant changes result mainly from planned efforts to increase efficiency. Because nearly complete rational administrative control is assumed, any recognized departures from rationality are attributed to random mistakes, ignorance, miscalculation, or other impediments to rationality.

There are a number of considerations which the model ignores and, in fact, obscures. First, attempts to rationalize the organization may obscure the less formal and less rational elements of organization that also contribute to its effectiveness. The rational attitude that "nothing is sacred" in organization also ignores the fact that people become emotionally involved in the established ways of doing things, problems of organization arise precisely because the organization becomes a sacred end in itself. Nor do executives, in fact, have complete control over the organization because it is dependent upon outside forces which divert the organization persistently from its long-range goals.

The rational model is grounded in a biological model of society that underlies the structural-functional view of society. The model rests on the complacent belief that "good" organizations are essentially harmonious and static, an unmistakably selective perception of the way organizations operate. It is assumed that societies exist in a state of harmonious equilibrium maintained by the consensus of their members, and that conflict, irregularity, change, and dissent are, accordingly a "sickness" which disrupts the harmony. This view of conflict as a disease having primarily "dissociating and dysfunctional consequences" is sharply criticized as Utopian by Dharendorf in an essay with a provocative title, "Out of Utopia." His observations merit extensive reflection by persons interested in building an administrative theory. He observes that all Utopias, from Plato's Republic to Orwell's brave new world of 1984, have several elements in common. First, they are all societies from which basic change is absent, with the exception of orderly change, or a "moving equilibrium," which occurs so uniformly throughout the society that it is never upsetting to anyone. Also, Utopias are uniformly consistent and based on a universal consensus in regard to prevailing values and institutional arrangements. In these perfectly agreeable societies there is a caste like relation between the leaders and the oppressed, who would never revolt against their superiors. Recalling that Socrates finally decided that justice really means that everyone does what is incumbent upon him. Dharendorf notes, with some disgust, that modern theorists have also discovered that justice means that everybody "plays his role." Although some writers add a clever touch of realism by inventing an individual non-conformist who is considered to be a pathological case, according to Dharendorf his only role is to highlight the inherent good of conforming. Finally, it is uniformly true that Utopias are isolated from all other communities. Since citizens of Utopias are seldom confronted with demands from the outside world, the society maintains complete control over its environment and complete autonomy to establish and fulfil its goals.

Conflict Model

Dharendorf observes that advocates of "empirical research" and defenders of abstract theory are stubbornly similar in one respect. They have both dispensed with the prime impulse of all science, the puzzlement over concrete intellectual problems, the simple curiosity to solve "the riddles of experience." Problems, as opposed to topics or fields of inquiry, exist because they are puzzling to the investigator. Their solution demonstrates, above all, critical examination of facts, observation, and testing which generates new problems. Dharendorf believes that this loss of problem consciousness explains the Utopian state of modern theory.

One of the carious riddles of society concerns the problem of "social glue," or in other words: what holds organizations together. Why do people join organizations and "play" roles. If the blinds of organization are personal harmony and group consensus, why do they persist despite the facts of organized resistance, internal friction, intrinsic competition, and sometimes radical cleavages that characterize organizations. It is unreasonable to dismiss so common a phenomenon as conflict as "accidental" and "exceptional" to the normal process. On the contrary, perhaps it is not the presence, but the absence of conflict that constitutes the surprising and the abnormal. At the very least, what seems to be called for is a model of organization in which power and power conflict have a central place. It is proposed that power has a vital place in the maintenance of social order as consensus, and that conflict itself, as a natural adjunct of power relationships, provides a form of cohesiveness. Some premises of a conflict theory of organization follow:

1. The Group Nature of Conflict. Contrary to a popular view, conflict is not purely personal, or the subjective expression of individual psyches. Conflict is a group phenomenon and extends beyond the subjective attitudes of persons as group members. Barnard points out, for example, that just as a thousand loves between soldiers and enemy women is not equal to peace, so a dozen disputes between American tourists and French cab drivers is not equivalent to a French-American conflict; parties in conflict may even display affection toward one another, as in the cases of conflict between the sexes or age groups and the numerous wars fought by "peace-loving" people. Since conflict can exist independently of personal hostility, personal attitudes reveal little about group relations. Moreover, Barnard maintains that improving interpersonal relations by "getting people together" (as in the comprehensive school) does not necessarily reduce conflicts which are based on institutional differences (for example, race), and in cases where enemies definitely have something to fight about, getting them together may simply expose their basic differences and drive them to their extremes.

2. Cultural Relativism. Historically the "good" people have usually fought the "good." Nations participating on each side in the religious crusades claimed religious justification. Modern nations each establish elaborate moral justifications for their inhumane acts of violence. The neighbours who dispute their property are likely to be "good" citizens, just as "progressive" educators and "essentialists" and authoritarians" are equally "good" people. That is, the "good" man is generally the supporters of his own groups' values, while the "bad" man is usually on the opposing side. Thus, the problem is not which side is "good," but what the fight is all about.

3. An Organization is a Balance of Power. What is defined as "good" may have had a long history of struggle for acceptance, as, for example, did Christianity, which was at one time the religion of a downcast minority. In this sense, the world, a society, or an organization, as each exists, is the outcome of historical power struggles and is the remnant of resulting animosities. All organizations are subject to some incipient cleavages on the basis of their previous history. Since the defeat of an idea or of a group seldom requires complete annihilation, scars remain which provide the basis for cleavage in new conflicts. Playground fights are not entirely due to personality problems; those fighting may represent different community groups and families in conflict-social classes, racial, religious and ethnic groups. Like school-boys' fights, the more sophisticated battles between their parents, teachers, administrators and other school personnel, often reflect deep-seated animosities nourished by past events.

4. Conflicts Create Cooperation. Cooperation and conflict are not polar opposites, but are in fact closely related group processes; conflict between groups promotes cooperation within groups. Because groups must cooperate intensively in order to wage conflict, the cohesiveness and discipline of a group may be indicative of impending disputes with another group. Also, as new conflicts occur, new forms of cooperation emerge. For example, competing groups within a school system will nevertheless work together when their mutual interest is jeopardized by outside groups. Superintendents intentionally employ this principle when they cast the blame for certain internal problems onto the school board. This alternating conflict and cooperation between groups, which can take place among the same individual, provides an element of unpredictability and flux in the organizational structure.

5. Groups Must be Visible to Conflict. Conflicts cannot occur between groups that are not indentifiable; each side in a conflict must have some physical or symbolic identity. This requirement of visibility helps to explain why certain minority groups which are in opposition to the established order; deliberately maintain a uniquely characteristic appearance. Members of such groups who do not maintain the symbols are outcast by the group, not so much because their acts are mortal sins.

6. Conflict is Sustained by Ideology. Symbolic identities have their highest expression in the statements of ideologies justifying the group's position in conflict. For example, each side of the 'town-and-gown" fights between colleges and their communities around the country has its rationale or its justification. Professors are viewed as potentially dangerous liberals of an impractical bent by a nation that is grossly anti-intellectual, while many professors delight in thinking of laymen as crass, unsophisticated, conservative materialists. The ideology of local democratic control over the schools bolsters resistance to consolidation or to any interference in local affairs from state departments of education, while state departments justify their interference on the basis of elaborate ideologies about raising the standards of education, benevolence, and professional expertise.

(a) ***The Doctrine of Equality.*** Conant's basic value premise is equality of opportunity, not equality of reward. Consequently, he emphasizes that there should be a minimum of social class distinction to facilitate social mobility. Yet, while he is interested in maintaining an open class structure, he does not advocate homogeneity of social groups either, and he encourages diversity.

(b) ***Programmes of Education.*** Conant believes that education must train persons for a variety of disciplines. He would like to have a variety of programs, designed to benefit all types of students

and all types of intellectual abilities. He believes that specialized education should be at a relatively late age so that persons are not prematurely "forced" into a career pattern before their interests and abilities are known.

(c) ***Conceptualizations of Education.*** Conant perceives education in its pragmatic, utilitarian aspects. First, it is a way to implement a fluid social structure, providing a means of social mobility. Second, education for Conant is more than a way to train an elite; it is a way to train citizens to live in a democracy. He sees education, then, as a way to make democratic society work. This is most clearly seen in his exaltation of the "comprehensive" high school which he believes will develop mutual respect among persons of diverse backgrounds who attend.

(d) ***Interpretation.*** This brief-summary of the two positions should be sufficient to suggest for the reader two basic philosophical positions under controversy today in public education. From the standpoint of conflict theory. Nock and Conant are representatives of two identifiable groups in competition over a limited social value; their philosophies are used by groups in conflict as justifications. The middle class is being justified by Conant and the upper class has been justified by Nock. From this view, one function of education is to transmit a group's values to its young; it is a training programme for "new young warriors" to staff groups in conflict. Nock's distinction between education and training is illuminating. He defines training in terms of those subjects (science) which help to promote the social mobility of the middle class, and equal opportunity for all classes. Yet, it is equally obvious that "education" in Nock's terms also amounts to a training programme—the training of a cultural elite. Latin, Greek, and math are symbols of identification with the upper social class, the landed leisure class that once controlled the society and still struggle for survival against the newer commercial and industrial middle class.

7. Conflict Influences Goals. Due to conflicts which normally exist within and between organizations, some personnel have aims which are not expressed in the official statement of purposes. This situation nourishes a diversity of organizational goals and unplanned cleavages between departments which further compromise the original goals. The operating goals, consequently, are partly forged out of the conflict process. As a note of caution, perhaps the conflict model is too preoccupied with these spontaneous and unplanned developments of goals, but it is a pre-occupation which at least counteracts its systematic neglect in the rational model of organization.

The Implications

The important question at this point is not which model is more "real to life," but which raises the more significant questions. In the conflict model, "organization" is problematic. It calls for an investigation of organization as an initially "unnatural" state of affairs and forces the question to be asked; what causes organization? Answers to this question will provide answers to the question about the role of the school administrator.

Special Nature

School administration is viewed in this book from a general perspective on organizations. General principles of organization and conflict are borrowed from literature on other type of organizations. This does not imply, however, that problems of administration are unrelated to the type or organizational goals, the organization's complexity, and its degree of centralization and standardization. There are certain characteristics of education suggested by Campbell which make it a somewhat special case. Yet, it will be clear as they are far from denying the relevance of sociological perspective and conflict model, each special feature seems to support the critical relevance of the conflict model.

First education is a service that deals directly and intimately with people; perhaps this hardly makes education a belligerent enterprise. However, the school does things to people as well as for them; parents will be especially suspicious of some types of changes which may occur in their children. The conflict centres partly on which services the school is to render to a community with diverse interests and high hopes, and partly on the authority of the school to make that decision and to control the means of implementing it. Parents have exercised a long and, in some sense, legitimate control over administrative decisions which, however, is also legally delegated to the school boards and which is often usurped by professional doctrines of authority.

Second, the development of a critical attitude is a central part of most educational philosophies, and some objectivity is generally expected of the public school system. This analytical attitude, supported by ideologies of academic freedom, is sometimes directed toward highly valued aspects of society. Consequently, there always exists a remote possibility that schools will lead pupils to revolt against certain aspects of the established order which some members of the community uphold. Public sensitivity to this possibility increases interest in the school from outsiders who can exert sometimes overwhelming pressures. Teachers, children, parents, and administrators may differ on the utility of critical thinking in practice if not in philosophy.

Third, there are explosive impediments to accurate evaluation of the success of schools. Policy statements tend to be so abstract that they are useless in establishing criteria of success. What is "good citizenship?" Does it include critical attitudes toward the government or not? What are the criteria of good teaching? What is a "successful" student? Often many years are required before attitude changes effected by high schools are revealed in behaviour. This ambiguity in evaluating teaching success is less apparent in some phases of business, particularly in sales, where effectiveness can be measured in terms of sales volume and effectiveness of promotion campaigns. The actual criteria of success used by teachers and administrators have been left direction less by the ambiguity of goals and standards of success, and these criteria must be hammered out in practice from the different available expectations.

Fourth, education differs from other organizations in the structure of the forces that control it. School boards represent various special interests of the community and have almost complete legal control over school policies; school administrators have almost no legal status, and their job is subject to the school board's pleasure, which greatly impairs the administrator's control over his organization. He is forced to compete for the support of various special interest groups which attempt to influence school practices and he must often act as a mediator between them. Because these groups are inexperienced and untrained in education, the administrator may wish to resist some of their demands; but because they control his job, he may be in a poor position to do so.

Finally, the school's physical structure and organization merit special attention. Unlike many organizations, such as the hospital, the school cannot be understood as a separate unit, for it is part of a system of units physically dispersed throughout the community and state. The fact that the superintendent's office is physically remote from the principal's office may be of some consequence for the development of unauthorized autonomy in some schools, problems of communication, and the kind of criteria used to evaluate teachers.

School administration is obviously, then, not identical to other forms of administration in all respects. The differences, however, should not be permitted to obscure the similarities; and in fact they may merely serve to highlight many of the same characteristics found in other modern organizations to which conflict models have demonstrated relevance. In any case the concepts that have proved faithful to us in studying complex organizations are those that have common rather than specific application.

Power and Authority

Organization is primarily supported by two types of force, power and authority. Power is sometimes conceived as the non-legitimate or illegitimate threat of force to achieve an end, while authority is the right to use force, which is granted either by the consensus of those over whom it is wielded, or by delegation from other authorities. Powe1, then will refer to the potential of force, and authority will refer to the right to exercise that force. Power is calibrated from minor influence at one extreme, to complete control at the other. While both power and authority involve the threat of force, force need not be actually applied in order to exert either power or authority.

Excessive display of authority may in fact dissipate power as repeated applications use up the available alternatives. Un-exercised power may also lose some of its threat, of course, but the more significant fact is that power is directly proportional to the number of alternatives available and is diminished when they are used. It is, for example, evident that persons who are willing to use illegal and unethical alternatives have more power than those who feel constrained by legal and ethical principles. Similarly, within the legal and ethical limits, each application of power consumes an alternative and simultaneously commits the organization to a line of action which further restricts its alternatives in the future. For example, in March, before the annual contracts have been signed, principals have a source of power over teachers that is not available in April after they have been signed.

A person may have authority without actually having the power to implement it. In fact, because power is a function of the alternatives available, authority and power may be inversely related. That is, the very legitimacy of authority constrains the kinds of alternatives that an authority may use in order to exercise its power. Authority is constrained by popular expectations, values, and traditions, which necessarily bind the use of power. The restraints on power that accompany authorization are apparent in the fact that fraud and bribery are very effective kinds of power which are precluded to persons in authority. The power of the principal to fire incompetents is similarly constrained by the existing community sentiments toward the incompetent, opinions of his colleagues, and humanitarian concern about how it will affect his personal life. The number of persons who can be demoted or negatively treated by the chief executive in anyone year is limited at some point resistance will develop. Therefore, the availability of each negative alternative is diminished every time it is used. Moreover the way that the principal handles a particular incompetent will set a precedent that in turn restricts the alternatives which are proper for dealing with incompetents in the future.

To summarize, power is based on the ability to control rewards an action which may be seen as a threat, to be effective, it must be used occasionally. However, just as power increases as the range of alternatives increases, it diminishes as alternatives are actually consumed, for each application sets a precedent which precludes other alternatives. Authorized power is regulated by public opinion or organizational consensus. In the long run, though, there seems to be a tendency for those who exercise sheer power to gain public respect and legitimacy over a period of time.

Official and Informal Structures

Uses of authority of power form several distinct structures within organizations. A structure includes both a set of positions which prescribe broad functions and specific duties incumbents, and a system of norms which regulate the relationship between incumbents of different positions. Official positions in organizations will be referred to as offices. Each office constitutes a system of jobs, or roles, which prescribe the responsibilities (rights and obligations) of that office with respect to other offices in the system. Accordingly, the superintendent's office cannot be understood apart from the responsibilities of other offices in the system, including the roles of classroom teachers.

Although the term structure implies a stable pattern of relationships, it may be viewed as a variable; organizations can be more or less structured in several respects. The most structured system is the official authority system. The official obligation of superintendents is to provide facilities for teachers and to influence their direction; the principal is responsible for staffing and coordinating classrooms; the teacher is supposed to instill knowledge and values in pupils without showing favoritism, and so on. There are, however, contradictions even within the official system. Authority may have several bases. It may stem from traditional rights to make decisions, it may be delegated by political powers vested with legal and institutional authority, it may be assumed by mutual agreement among personnel, or it may be assumed by some individual because of a special competence.

Moreover, there are competing systems in the school, besides the official one, which create even further variability in the extent to which the overall system can be said to be 'structured' or coordinated. These competing systems give rise to several different informal authority structures in addition to the legal and official ones. Informal leaders develop among teachers on the basis of the esteem of their colleagues. Since the authority arising from these unofficial sources is independent of the legal-official structure, it in effect constitutes a separate system of authority—the informal authority structure. The informal authority structure is intermediate between the official structure and the informal power structure. In the sense that such uses of power are not officially authorized, they technically constitute a power structure, yet, in the sense that they are authorized by group opinions, they are authority structures.

Systems of completely unauthorized power, or power structures, complicate the picture still further. Informal power structures exits simultaneously with, yet independently of the informal authority structures, being unauthorized even by mutual consent of colleagues.

To summarize, there is a structural connection between authority and power, respectively, the official and the informal organizations which they underlie. It is a crude relationship since some facets of the informal structure are authorized informally, and because competing bases of legitimization exist which are decided by power conflicts. Because authority relationships are infinitely more predictable than power relations, which by definition may exist outside the normal structure of expectancy and group control, authority is an understandably popular approach to organizational theory and planning. However, because structure is a variable and because there are a variety of structures (some based on unstable power relations), change and instability must be recognized as inherent to organizations.

Status and Office

It is by now a truism that the official and informal

structures of an organization are drastically influenced by the society in which they exist. The statement, nevertheless, is a reminder that administration cannot be viewed apart from the general status system of the society and the manner in which the status is translated into organizational practices. The concept of status refers to a position in the general society; it parallels the term office, which designates positions within a particular organization.

Contradictions between status and office are also sources of dilemmas. For example, age has a different meaning within the status system of the broader society and the official system of the school. For, while it may be officially proclaimed that ability is the only important consideration for promotion, within the school age is important. Because responsibility is supposed to be relegated to older persons, a young principal or superintendent in command of older persons can create a problem. Female high school principals who command a predominantly male staff may create a similar dilemma.

Institution and Organization

Statuses and offices comprise different "social orders." Offices constitute the fundamental element of an organization, while statuses are the basis of social institutions. Together, the offices constitute the responsibilities of the school system, its jobs, or its "roles," which outline rights and duties with respect to other offices. They comprise, in other words, the organizational structure providing the organization's regularity and stability; conflicts between offices provide its dynamic quality as well.

Organization behaviour is to be understood in terms of offices rather than exclusively in terms of members' personality characteristics. Modern man lives in a "contract" society in which people react to each other without knowledge of their personalities. Administrators do business with teachers, contractors, students, and parents, sometimes with almost no knowledge of their personal characteristics, yet with relative ease and success because people are expected to behave according to their status. Little insecurity is felt by school officials when they entrust the schools' monies to bank tellers who may be virtual strangers, because even though the teller may nave dishonest tendencies, he will nevertheless tend to conform to the obligations of his office rather than give in to his personal inclinations. Similarly, teachers may be personally prejudiced against Negroes, but strive to be equalitarian with Negro students in schools where discrimination is condemned, and, conversely, personally unprejudiced teachers may be forced to racially discriminate in some systems.

While the official system is not determined primarily by the personalities of those who are in it, it is primarily affected by the institutional system that underlies it. The institutional "order" consist primarily of the statuses that compose each institution. Institutions are rules that link cultural values to specific situations. They have no official name and location as organizations do, and institutions are more abstract than organizations, comprised of values and rules that transcend a location and specify the general organizational forms.

Thus, the job of "educator" is straightforward; he is to develop in children knowledge and character. But what is distinct about the institutional order is that there may be inconsistent expectations among institutions. A "good family man," for example, is expected to spend his evenings at home with his family, but the good community citizen is expected to spend his time working on community projects, and the good businessman is expected to use his evenings to work overtime and "get ahead." The point then is this: a single institution, such as education, is implemented in a number of different organizations besides the schools, such as businesses and the military, all of which have educational programmes; and a single organization, such as a particular school, is comprised of a variety of often inconsistent institutional statuses. The job of a teacher at secondary school is hardly described simply by her status as an educator; that job is comprised of a variety of institutions, among them business, politics, religion, and so on. In addition to teaching the children, she is to keep attendance records, chaperone parties, sell war bonds, encourage patriotic and religious devotion, and provide spiritual and vocational guidance. In these activities, educational values must be compromised with recreational, business, patriotic, religious, and other institutions in the work place. The "official" job then, comprised of a variety of institutions, is an arena of institutional conflict where compromises among political, religious, business, educational, and other value systems are carved out of the daily work routine. In the process, educational ideals are sometimes implemented, sometimes usurped; by other institutional means. This implies that the character of the public schools cannot be understood solely in terms of educational principles and philosophies, but must be understood within the context of the broader institutional order, including politics, business, religion, and other basic value systems. It also means that the official system is inherently one of conflict, the same conflict that persists in the more abstract institutional order.

Professional and Bureaucratic Orientations

The dilemmas of employed professional constitute a peculiar form of the local-cosmopolitan dilemma. The bureaucratic employee is expected to reserve his primary loyalty for the school where he is locally employed, particularly to its administration. The professionally oriented teacher, on the other hand, will probably be more influenced by the stands taken on issues by professional society, by professors at influential training centres, and by colleagues across the country. Conflicts in the professional and employee orientations can become particularly acute when the issue involves racial integration, school consolidation, or relative importance of seniority and merit.

The Commitment

Although exercised by individuals, power and authority describe characteristics of the organization. Commitment and involvement, however, provide a parallel set of concepts which describe the power system from the standpoint of the individuals in it. While commitment and involvement tend to be correlated processes, they can be distinguished analytically. Considering the extremes, a person is completely "involved" when he does something solely because of personal desire without any formal obligation to do it. While there is an element of compulsion implicit in a commitment, it arises largely from the ethical and social pressures from precedented acts rather than from threat of direct force.

These concepts are useful in analyzing the strategies by which individuals and organizational leaders handle their problems. In complex organization, persons often must do what they dislike in order to obtain their preferences. As a result a person may commit himself to something and be involved with an entirely different matter. In other words, people exchange obligations for rights. Their life becomes a dynamic balance of commitment and involvement.

The concept of commitment is also useful for the analysis of power, which, as indicated, is a function of the number of available alternatives. Every major commitment consumes one or more alternatives by binding the organization to an irrevocable line of action. Moreover, every decision creates still other commitments, ones that are often unforeseen. Informal commitments usually accompany the formal ones.

These unforeseen and compulsory types of commitments create considerable institutional drift from long-range goals. Selznick cites two sources of these strains between actual and operating goals. First, the daily minor decisions can lead the organization in directions it did not set out to travel. Old techniques of administration and teaching have a way of becoming sacred; thus, the goal of efficiency may actually be subverted by a seemingly minor decision to hire a tradition-directed accountant when planning to mechanize the records-keeping system. Second, drift is partly a consequence of a limited administrative; perspective that naturally occurs because administrators tend to stress rationality and formal organizational goals. In stressing the rational formal goals, unintended outcomes of decisions on informal goals tend to be overlooked, or are considered to be irrelevant because they are logically irrelevant.

The concept of commitment, then, implies a strategy of organization as well as individuals. The act of commitment is potentially an act of change which may eventually affect the organization's structure and goals. There is a need for organizational theorists to study this class of strategies, for the notion of commitment as a strategy calls attention to the simultaneous structure and change that constitutes the science of administration. The view stresses the flexibility of organizational structure and helps to offset some of the traditional emphasis on structure and goals as "given" qualities. It suggests the feasibility of viewing organization as a development over time by analyzing its strategic acts. The decision-making process is a particularly important crux of such analyses.

The analysis of organizational process had been so neglected, and the need for new departures so urgent, that there is some justification for taking the opposite viewpoints that process, strategy, and sheer "accident" are the "normal" states of organization, and structure is the "abnormal" state. Pursuit of such a view would require special conceptual tools. A few of the most promising of these tools include interplay, cooperation, and reciprocity. Interplay stresses the strategic character of organizational decision-making. It is a tactical relationship wherein the action of one person depends on the unknown outcome of a previous act; an administrator's decision to fire or retain a teacher, for example, depends in part on anticipated community reaction. Reciprocity refers to the norm of exchanging favours. Persons may often engage in conduct that is not personally approved by them, but which promises the fulfilment of obligation or the return of a favour. Co-optation refers to type of compromise in which an opponent is incorporated into the leadership structure of a group in order to control him better; some control over organizational affairs is sacrificed in exchange for greater control over the opponent. These concepts describe some of the types of commitments by which organizations are guided and compromized.

Our purpose is to communicate with each other to try to develop useful theory in educational administration. A seminar in which professors of educational administration and social scientists work together is salutary; it illustrates the progress made in the past decade progress characterized by a marked change of emphasis in the training of administrators.

***

5

Educational Planning and Difficulties

According to the Kothari Commission, in India the problem of educational planning means simply that we need to evolve a national policy in the educational sphere while, according to our Constitution, education is a state subject, and consequently, educational officials at various levels take decisions on all of its varied aspects. The task before us is not simple, and we also do not have much experience to guide us. Hence, we will have to evolve our own techniques, and change, modify and improve them as we go along.

The following are the elements of a comprehensive educational plan which have to be improved in order to overcome the problems that arise in the educational sphere:

1. Creation of literature in the modern Indian languages, which is necessary for making these languages the medium of instruction at the university level.
2. Preparation of text-books for schools and help-materials for teaching and study.
3. Educational Research.
4. Improvements in the system of examination.
5. Arrangements for the in-service training of teachers and officials of the education department.

6. Increase in the contact with guardians and the local community.
7. Improvements in the methods of supervision.
8. Provision of progressive schemes for brilliant students and programmes of special assistance to backward students.

Difficulties on Way

The results of education can be good only if educational planning is successful. In our country, educational planning faces the following obstacles:

1. Excessive emphasis upon enrolment and expenditure.
2. Decentralisation of efforts.
3. Absence of adequate evaluation and research.
4. Indifference towards accepting clearly defined paths of action.
5. Failure to initiate programmes of superior quality.
6. Weakness of the educational planning mechanism.

The Planning Commission's Working Group on education has identified the following causes of the failure of planning:

1. Administration of the police kind, obsolete methods, inadequate resources, increased responsibilities of development, and untrained, incapable and inadequate staff.
2. Lack of attraction for trained individuals; tradition of making appointments from above; absence of any system of in-service training; excessive emphasis upon individual and financial administration. There is need for a revolutionary change in the nature and structure of the states department of education.

Instead of functioning as groups of individuals concerned with grants, statistics, financial permission, transfers, appointments, study of complaints, etc., these groups have to become organizations of educationists which possess the imagination to visualize the objectives of educational reconstruction, which are sensitive enough to recognize quickly the needs and demands of people immediately, which can prepare satisfactory plans for reconstruction and implement them successfully, which can fulfil the roles of friends, philosophers and guides for the teachers as well as students and their guardians.

3. Cooperation and harmony with other governmental departments and non-governmental agencies is weak and ineffective.

4. Proper utilisation of resources is hindered because of lack of resources, lack of extension schemes, delays in obtaining financial clearance, changes in the proposed amounts or corrupt activities.

4. The entire society is responsible for making the educational plan successful. Till the present, there is no effective system for establishing contact between teachers, students, guardians educational administrators and the rest of society, though the existence of such a system is a prime necessity.

6. Political pressures are often seen working powerfully in the appointment and transfer of teachers, setting up of new institutions and location of schools. The same pressures also influence and modify approved schemes.

7. Wherever-suitable leadership has been found lacking, democratic decentralisation has led either to the obstruction of educational schemes or a complete

and destructive change in their very nature. Local influences and force often create problems for the teachers.

8. The thought that goes into making a-budget or preparing in a plan is the equivalent of a kind of evaluation. Evaluation is made from time to time. The discussion in the organizations of teachers, the press and the legislative assemblies are also forms of evaluation. But, hardly any efforts have been made so far towards introducing a systematic and formal mode of evaluation by individuals directly involved in education.

In view of these factors, the Working Group felt constrained to say that comprehensive educational plans, keeping in view every aspect of education, should be prepared. The existing situation is that the states' departments of education thrust the responsibility for planning on certain officials, who then prepare plans and programmes without getting into touch with anyone. Specialists, teachers, organizations of teachers, or educational officials of the district level make no contribution to such plans. Besides, these plans are full of statistics about goals of appointments and expenses, while other much more important aspects of education are completely neglected.

Detailed schemes and blue-prints are also required for the successful implementation of a plan. No attention is paid to this fact. The Working Group's view is that educational programmes should be treated in the same way in which projects concerning irrigation, industry or power are treated. We should see not merely the clarity of objectives; we must also seek to ensure the achievement of these objectives by considering the time division, need for preparatory work, materials expenditure needed for creating the necessary skills and motivation and administrative requirements, and then by to harmonize them with the time available and conditions existing. At present, there is a complete absence of such projects.

It seems that detailed thinking does not go into the preparing of plans by the education ministry and the Planning Commission, and after plans are once prepared, re-thinking occurs only after a year has passed.

It seems that detailed thinking does not go into the preparing of plans by the education ministry and the Planning Commission, and after plans are once prepared, re-thinking occurs only after a year has passed. Assessments are hardly ever made. Besides, the various agencies looking after education also lack coordination among themselves. At the national level, various ministries, such as food, agriculture, labour, social welfare, home, etc, are also involved in educational planning. Similar agencies exist in the states also, but the coordination among them is quite weak.

The Remedies

It is true that education is the state's responsibility, but it cannot be denied that the nation has an equal responsibility as well as stake in the success of education. Hence, the states and the centre should be regarded as equal partners in education. There are three main agencies of education—*(i)* the central government, *(ii)* the state governments, and *(iii)* local bodies and voluntary organizations. Besides, it is evident that *(a)* school education involves the partnership of the local government and the state government, and *(b)* higher education is conducted through the partnership of the state and central governments. A balance can be struck between complete centralization or decentralization after these truths are recognized and accepted.

The Working Group has offered the following suggestions for making educational planning successful:

Preparation of Comprehensive Educational Plans. Allocation of resources is all that is actually being done in the name of formulating plans. A comprehensive educational plan is inclusive of the existing situation in education, the objectives, of education, the steps to be taken for achieving these objects, all programmes, those which involve no expenditure or those for which expenditure has to be reduced, etc.

Basis of the Process of Planning. The second necessary reform relates to giving the planning process a wider basis and decentralizing it, as well as bringing about coordination between the institution, district, state and centre. This will produce a wide range of advantages.

Introduction of Institutional Plans. The basic principle of this new technique will be institutional plans, *i.e.,* plans prepared by the schools themselves. At the school level, plans have to be formulated by considering what can be done within the available resources or by adding a little to them. Good schools in particular should work in this direction.

Work can be started in the states on the basis of the following suggestions:

1. An essential condition for granting recognition and aid should be that each school should prepare a five-year plan, as well as annual plans, for its own development.
2. These plans should also become the basis of inspection.
3. The department of educational should provide some guidelines in the preparation of the school's plan which should be clearly in consonance with the state's policy on education.
4. Long-term plans will run concurrently with the state's five-year plans. Schools will re-open at the

fixed time, though students will attend school a week latter. During this period, the teachers will consider every aspect of teaching and prepare plans for the forthcoming session.

5. The principals of institutions should prepare plans according to the directives of the department.
6. The state educational institution should train principals as well as inspectors.
7. Inspectors should receive detailed information about plans and evaluation well in advance.
8. Inspectors often compel schools to adopt many schemes simultaneously. For this, it is essential that the schemes should be limited in range, and they should be completed before others are taken up.
9. All the related agencies-teachers, students, society, guardians, principal, the management committee, etc., should participate in the preparation of the plan.

We should remember that education is a never ending or inexhaustible source of personal satisfaction. It is related directly to the nation's social and economic development. If education is systematically initiated at every level, and if it is intimately related to national programme, the pace of social and economic development increases.

Developmental Plans

While reflecting upon institutional planning, we are faced with the following questions: *(a)* What are your objectives? *(b)* Is our purpose to work for the achievement of new objectives? *(c)* Do we want to bring about a change in individuals? *(d)* Is it our purpose to replace the old patterns with fresh ones? These questions imply that our thinking on the issue should be clear. The function of institutional planning is to keep an institution occupied in the search for the best possible results in the existing social environment.

In the context of formulating a plan with clear objectives for any institution, it is necessary to reflect upon the existing circumstances. One cannot turn away from the realities of life and society. We must overlook the fact that our universities are tradition bound and that they have to work according to the directives of the department of education. It is the department which formulates the curriculum and also issues orders about its implementation. Thus, if we can still think of an imaginative plan for a particular institution, despite the existence of these circumstances, it must necessarily be appreciated.

In order to prepare an educational plan for a single institution, it is necessary to consider the following bases:

1. Achievement of the best possible results in the given social and physical environment.
2. Reform and progress in technique, materials, resources, etc.
3. Generating a suitable atmosphere for the development of creativity.
4. Making the best use of the talents of the students and teachers.
5. Encouraging mutual cooperation without injuring freedom of thought and action.
6. Recognition of innate powers, their use, encouragement of efforts and leadership.
7. Achieving the maximum utilization of building, laboratories, libraries and other resources.
8. Practising self-service and self-achievement.

The Working Group of the Planning Commission has suggested the following means of bringing Success to the plans of schools:

1. The states' departments of education will have to begin to think a new In order to recognize or identify good schools and grant them greater aid as well as freedom to guide the weaker schools towards improvement and also to encourage competitiveness, creativity and experimentation amongst teachers and students. Instead of uniformity and rigidity, it will be necessary to adopt an approach which is dynamic and flexible.

2. The schools themselves should try to secure the means needed for their development. The best steps in this direction would be *(i)* the cooperation of local officials, guardians and the local community, *(ii)* a change in the method of giving grants in order to encourage superiority, and *(iii)* establishment of experimental schools and autonomous colleges.

3. Transfers of teachers in government schools should be reduced to a minimum. Organizing committees or boards of governors should be created, and in these the teachers should have an important voice, so that their commitment should be to the institution, and not merely to their cadre. Such a situation does not exist in private institutions, and hence they should make efforts to attract the best teachers towards themselves.

4. Teachers have necessarily to shoulder the leadership in the formulation and implementation of institutional plans. Among primary schools, there exists the peculiar problem of single-teacher institutions. For such cases, all institutions within a radius of three to five miles will beat the higher

secondary school as the centre, and function as a school complex, and their institutional plan will also be a collective one. From the viewpoint of organization, each complex should be treated as a unit. At the secondary school level, the form of principals will work to achieve cooperation from the nearest college or university and to ensure mutual cooperation. A complex can also be created by linking a college or even a department of a university with a group of secondary schools.

5. It is necessary to initiate cooperation and mutual dialogue between schools and colleges, instead of allowing them to throw allegations at each other. School complexes can be of tremendous advantage in this sphere.

6. Transfers can help each other in the framing and implementation of plans even through the method of Panel Inspection. The panel can consist of some selected teachers and principals who can give the benefit of their experience and knowledge to other institutions, apart from their own, by giving a little extra time.

7. Colleges will, in general, not have much difficulty in preparing their own plans, but they can seek the guidance of the university. The universities, too, will frame their own plans for this purpose, in keeping with the suggestions of the Education Commission, they will create their own 'academic planning boards.'

Different Steps. Institutional planning operates at three levels: (1) District, (2) State and (3) National.

District Level Plans. Accepting the district as the fundamental unit of planning, development and administration, work is to be initiated in some districts in the next year itself. It is to be introduced in every district by the end of the sixth five year plan. Today, the expenditure on education in a single district is more than the total expenditure in India in 1882. The educational plan of a district should comprehend all educational activity below the level of university education-pre-primary, primary, secondary and vocational. Towns with a population of a lakh or more can also have their separate plans, in which the municipal boards should also offer cooperation.

State Level Plans. Plans at the state level have to become the centre of gravity of the entire planning process, and for this purpose, it is essential that every state department of education must have a powerful and effective planning wing. For the near future, the following programmes have been suggested for immediate implementation: *(i)* Evaluation of the development from independence till the present, *(ii)* formulation of a long-term plan for fifteen or twenty years, publication of a white paper on the subject, and giving it a final shape in the light of the suggestions received, *(iii)* framing of an Education Act.

National Plans. At the national level, the government of India has suggested the formulation of a national educational policy which should be reviewed every five years. National plans will be based on this national policy. Their main elements will be the following: *(i)* the synthesizing element of framing a national plan based on all state-plans, *(ii)* coordinated action on the national plan by the centre as well as the states, *(iii)* central programmes to be implemented either by constitutional directives or the assent of the states. It will be the Centre's responsibility to produce a plan which does away with regional differences, which is balanced, and which is suited for a long-term period for this purpose, special national programmes within the overall national plan will have to be evolved.

The Dual Process of Plan Formulation. Planning has to be done both from above and from below. It is necessary to have two time-tables in the planning process. For example, guidelines and hints about the temporary allocation of resources will flow from the central government to the state government, from the state government to the district level officials and institutions. In the reverse process, the institutions will prepare their own plans in the light of the information given. They will indicate the plans they can implement with the given resources, and what they may be able to do if more resources are made available, etc.

Contribution of Teachers. Teachers are expected to cooperate intimately and effectively in educational plans. Theoretically, this does not appear to be an unusual idea, but in effect, it has been implemented so far because of the following four factors: *(i)* The government has never shown any interest in this, and in fact the government has never understood either this problem or its importance. *(ii)* We have, as yet, never seen even a dream of any institutional organization which makes it possible for teachers to participate in the formulation and implementation of educational plan. *(iii)* There are so many differences among the various categories of teachers that the whole profession has been weakened, and consequently the teacher's capacity to contribute to educational planning is almost destroyed. *(iv)* Teachers are also lacking in specialisation and leadership, besides which they have adopted an attitude of indifference towards the problems of education planning. These four difficulties have to be overcome in order to benefit education by raising the status of teachers, which can be done by giving them the leadership in educational planning and development.

For this, the following suggestions have been offered:

(a) School-planning should be introduced in every school.

(b) At the district level, there should be an advisory board council of teachers on which every teacher organization of the district should have representation. It should be consulted in every matter pertaining to educational planning and development.

(c) Similar advisory boards should also be created at the, state level, and these should be called joint teachers' councils.

(d) The government should declare, without any reservations and conditions, that it wishes to hand over the leadership in matters of educational planning to the teachers, and, that the responsibility for helping in this work and collecting the necessary resources will fall upon the department of education. Such a declaration will influence the attitudes of departmental officials as well as teachers and lead to the creation of a suitable environment which is essential for the success of this entire programme.

(e) The central ministry of education should establish a national committee of teachers on which every teacher organization of the national level should be represented. In planning and development matters, this committee should be consulted, as is to be done at the district and state levels.

(f) Efforts must be made to win the cooperation of the teachers in administrative activities relating to the school as well as other matters.

(g) The teachers themselves should develop an interest in planning. It is unfortunate that teachers have neglected this important aspect of their vocation. Teachers organizations have shown no interest in the past three five-year plans and three annual plans. They have not indulged in any profound criticism or analysis, though it is expected of them that they would not only subject the government's plans to criticism, but also offer a parallel plan of their own, so that the people may have an opportunity for a comparative study.

(h) If teachers of all categories unite and form a single, organized community, their contribution to educational administration can become more effective. For this, the first thing necessary is a change of attitude. At present, the teaching profession is divided into a number of discrete units which, it appears, visit their own classrooms individually without ever entering into a working relationship. It is obvious that there is no place for such an alienated outworn attitude in the new India that we dream of, a country with a social system based on equality, freedom, justice and the dignity of the individual. The community of teachers is one, and all within it are fundamentally equal.

(i) Teachers will also have to develop the necessary skills for planning; both individuals and in groups, through their organizations. Of course, it is true that this will happen only when the plan for decentralisation outlined earlier is implemented and teachers are asked to cooperate.

(j) In order to generate a commitment among the teachers for the institutions in which they teach, it is essential for them to have an effective voice in its administration. Suitable efforts for this will have to be made in private as well as governmental institutions.

Training. It is necessary to train all individuals concerned with the formulation and implementation of plans. Besides, some selected individuals must also be specially trained for formulating and implementing certain specialized projects. A detailed document should be prepared for each scheme, showing the objectives, period of work, finance, individuals involved, description of resources, arrangements for coordination, a detailed time division plan, made of evaluation, preparatory work, etc. This task is undoubtedly difficult, and the specialists available will also be few. Hence, the Asian Educational Planning and Administration Institution can be entrusted with providing help in this sphere.

Eradication of the Stress on Money. Every effort should be made to get rid of the stress on money in educational plans. If we imagine that surplus funds will help us to end every conceivable problem in education, the idea only indicates our naivete. After spending substantial amounts of money we have succeeded in expanding the general system of education and in creating new institutions, better scales of pay for teachers, more teaching, putting up more buildings, and expansion of resources. However, those improvements which were not related with finance have met with limited success only. We have almost completely failed in the growth of adult literacy or in preventing wastages and stagnation in primary education. The enrolment at the university and secondary level has not decreased. No noticeable progress in the schemes for qualitative Improvement has been noted. For all these activities, what is needed is more and better human resources, not more money. In the sphere of human efforts, our work has been unsatisfactory. In rich country, the emphasis upon money may not mean a serious loss, but in a poor country like ours, this lavishness is intolerable. We can achieve success in our objectives if we adopt the following major programmes along with our other schemes:

Cost Consciousness. The money invested should not exceed the profit gained.

Intensive Use of Available Resources. Efforts should be made to derive the maximum profits from the existing investments, instead of seeking avenues for fresh investments.

Selective Technique. Instead of taking up numerous schemes simultaneously some selected schemes should be chosen on the basis of priorities.

Research on Inexpensive Techniques. Science should pay attention to this field.

Human Efforts. The vicious circle lack of education in a poor country itself becoming the cause of further poverty should be broken through enthusiastic and dedicated human effort.

Priorities. It is necessary to determine priorities at the national, state and local levels. Today, there is a tendency to think of everything in terms of the national level. Instead of this attitude, it would be better if, at the national level, priority is given only to some subjects of truly national importance. These can be treated as national schemes. In teaching, production of books and teaching of science can be treated as national schemes for the sixth plan. On these issues, the Centre should finalize decisions after consultation with the states. But once a decision has been taken, the states will compulsorily have to act upon them in the most potent and effective manner possible.

On most of the remaining issues, the states themselves must take their own decisions, and in accordance with local needs, determine the priorities. For instance, at the secondary level, the question of an educational fee can be taken up'. There is no need to seek uniformity at the national level in such matters. In many other matters, such as facilities in schools and non-teacher costs, priorities will have to be fixed at the local level, in consonance with local needs and the clearly defined rights and authority of the school or local, body, which should also have the necessary freedom to take decisions. There is no need to expect absolute uniformity in all districts. In some matters, freedom must be given even to the schools. Neither is there any need to accept complete uniformity and conformity in all schools of the same category. A system based on coordinated and rationally determined priorities separately determined, at the national, state and local levels will be far better than the prevailing system in which, so far, many decisions have been taken, even in matters of regional and national importance, without the least attention to local needs. Such a system has led to the complete obstruction of any tendency to take the initiative and bring improvements.

Reformative Steps. For the proper implementation of educational programmes, it is necessary to bring about improvements in educational administration on the basis of well-defined priorities. At present, the education department focuses its attention only upon maintaining organizational administration, with the result that the duty of developmental administration is not fulfilled at all. For this latter purpose, the departments of education should have full knowledge of educational programmes in all the states of our own country as well as the programmes initiated in foreign countries. Besides they should give suitable importance to all such programmes m their own educational planning, keeping in view the needs aspirations and ambitions of the people of their region. Such a developmental administration will possess the following characteristics:

1. Developmental administration accords equal importance to the twin aspects of quantitative and quantitative improvement in education. It makes continuously modifiable and improved schemes for the future, evaluates the experiences of the past and present, and simultaneously provides the administrators with ever increasing opportunities for increasing their professional skills.

2. Organizational administration is suitable for a static or slowly progressing society, because it always sticks to uniformity and insists on obedience to

rules. On the other hand, developmental administration concerns itself with the development of the individual in a rapidly changing society, and for this purpose, it does not hesitate to modify its own policy, if this is necessitated by circumstances.

3. The existing organizational administration soon becomes involved in its own web of ever-expanding rules and regulations, by laying excessive stress upon control. It is thus unable to spare a thought to progress or development. In contrast, developmental administration gives importance to the independence of teachers and institutions, expansion in extension services and guidance, experimentation, initiative and creativity, and encourages all of them.
4. Another drawback of organizational administration is that it creates the two classes of teachers and administrators, with greater benefits invariably flowing to the latter. This discrimination invariably has an adverse impact both upon the teacher and the teaching process, as well as development of education. In contrast, developmental administration invariably aims at healthy relations between the two classes so that both of them are able to fulfil their respective duties without coming into conflict with each other.
5. Developmental administration is completely democratic and decentralized. As is the case of organizational administration, it has no place for the centralization of power or the creation of a bureaucratic approach. Every individual, at every level, has the right to make rules, to work accordingly and to evaluate his activities.

Having been accustomed to organizational administration for almost centuries it now appears difficult to adopt developmental administration. Even today, our administration spends almost the whole of its time in the appointment of workers, their transfers, promotions and investigation into anonymous complaints and allegations. Whatever time does remain is spent in sorting out financial complications. The consequence of this is that the department soon loses all touch with society, and it turns into an isolated tower standing in a waste land. In order to introduce developmental administration, we will first have to overcome these drawbacks. The suggestions for the improvement of educational administration are based on our assumption that the central and state governments are faced with the major task of making the objectives of education determined by the governments themselves.

The outstanding purpose or aim of educational administration is—improvements in educational services. This should be done at the state and central levels. It was with this in view that the suggestion for an Indian Educational Service was mooted, but, for a variety of reasons it was never implemented. Hence, it has become necessary to think of some other means of achieving the necessary goal. In this connection, the following measures are suggested:

1. An educational advisory service should be established. A service of this kind, associated with the ministry of education, suffers from many drawbacks, the main one being that its members are out of touch with existing realities, since they never have an opportunity to work in the practical field. The following programmes can be adopted for overcoming this weakness.

   (a) All the posts under the government of India requiring educational expertise as well as such voluntary organizations such as the Central Schools Organization should be combined under this. If possible, the states desirous of joining the unit may be allowed to do so.

(b) The officials of the states' departments of education, principals of schools, vice-chancellors of universities and famous educationists should be appointed to the posts of additional educational advisors. Such appointments should be made only for five years, though they may be extended for another 5 years under exceptional circumstances.

(c) Some posts in the central ministry of education should be reserved for officials nominated by the state governments. In exchange, some officials of the central ministry should be appointed in the states' departments of education. This policy will benefit both the Centre and the states. Officials from the central ministry will get an opportunity to increase their knowledge and experience about the actual conditions existing in the states, and also to make their own attitudes more liberal, while the states will benefit from the diverse and wide experience of the central government's educationists.

2. For the improvement of the states' departments of education, the following steps can be considered:

(i) The scales of pay of their officials should be improved.

(ii) The number of posts of inspectors should be increased to the extent necessary.

(iii) It is generally seen that the department fills the senior posts in the department by promoting junior officials. Even if direct recruitment is adopted for some posts, priority is still given to promotion of juniors. Consequently, fresh and enthusiastic individuals do not get any opportunity and the qualitative development of education suffers a setback.

(iv) The posts from the level of district education officer to the level of the director of education (where special qualifications and abilities are needed for framing policies and setting down rules) should be filled through offers of five-year contracts to able individuals working in schools, colleges and universities, though few such posts may be reserved for promoted individuals. Those employed on contract may be allowed to extent their contract for another five years, but only if their work in eminently satisfactory in the initial period.

Educational institutions should possess facilities whereby individuals with marked administrative talent may be enables to take up administrative jobs. On the other hand, administrative officials interested in teaching should be allowed opportunities for appointment in schools, colleges and universities.

Part Time Education. The second very significant programme far important is the provision of in-service education for educational administrators. This is even more important in view of the fact that the condition of the states' departments of education is truly pitiable at present. For this, the following steps have been suggested:

1. Each administrator or inspector should be required, on being first appointed, to complete a course of training, whose period and subject should be in accord with the posts held by the individual.
2. Education of this kind should have two purposes-one, to acquaint the officials from time to time with the state's educational policies, and two; to get an

opportunity to study improvements in education in India and abroad and to assess them in the light of the conditions in their own state. These officials should participate in conferences or seminars or workshops for at least a week twice a year. Such conferences should be organized, at the district or regional level, by the district officials, for the non-gazetted staff, while for the gazetted staff, they should be organized by the director of education.

3. Each department should regularly publish a newspaper or letter of the highest quality in order to acquaint its officials with the latest government policies as well as the least thinking in the educational sphere by leading educationists.

4. Officials of one state should be sent to other states for studying particular problem.

5. It is essential to have provisions for granting leave to those officials who wish to improve their knowledge or enter specialized studies at regular intervals. Six months leave can be granted after every six years for such purposes. In the past, India did have a system of further studies'. Similar schemes should now be evolved and adopted.

6. The ministry of education, the NCERT, and the Asian Educational Planning and Administration Institute should prepare a programme for in-service training, since such a programme can bring to the participants the knowledge, experience and guidance of experts and scholars in this field. The states' departments of education should allow their officials to participate in such programmes freely.

7. Both at the national and state levels, there should be arrangements by which officials of other departments concerned with education and its problems can be

kept in touch with latest ideas, and also be given training.

The Kothari Education Commission had suggested the establishment of a National College for the training of educational administrators. This is a very valuable suggestion, and it should be accepted and implemented in the present plan-period. Giving opportunities for improving professional qualifications is a good idea, but not all individuals are able to benefit from them. Hence, for encouragement, they should also be given incentives, such as promotions or increase in pay.

In view of the existing circumstances, it is essential that, within the next one or two years, massive programmes for the reorientation of our educational administrators should be taken up. In all such programmes organized at the national, regional or local level, the states and the Centre should cooperate with each other.

Perfect Schemes. The third programme for the improvement of educational administration concerns the proper organization of developmental work regarding schools and workers. For the last forty years, our attention has been focused upon the quantitative expansion of education, but the time is now ripe for concentrating upon its qualitative improvement. Many elements are important for this, for instance—the abilities of teachers, their devotion to duty, the commitment and motivation of students, an atmosphere conducive to truth and hard work, provision of facilities, a developed curriculum, dynamic methods of teaching and evaluation, research, good supervision and guidance work, and a favourable social climate. However, solving the problems of educational administration depends upon two factors: (1) school organization, and (2) supervision and guidance.

Before 1947, educational authorities were compelled to bear two burdens, those of administration as well as introduction of programmes of qualitative improvement. But after 1950, the work load of administrative activities upon these officers increased to such an extent that they had almost no time to spare for programme of qualitative improvement. Even as early as 15 years ago, it was felt that there was need for establishing special agencies to carry out developmental programmes. It was with this in view that such institutions as the Central Textbook Research Bureau, the Central Educational and Vocational Guidance Bureau, the National Audio-visual Education Institution, the National Basic Education Institute, the National Institute of Primary Education, Directorate for Extension Programmes in Secondary Education, Central English and Hindi Institutes, etc., were established. In a similar fashion, in the states, too, state education institutes audio-visual education institutes, educational and, vocational guidance institutes, evaluation organizations, state science teaching institutes, and the English institute, etc., came to be established.

It is beyond doubt that these agencies have succeeded in those states in which due attention was given to these two conditions, one, the department of education appointed its own highly qualified staff in these institutions, two, these officials were able to win the cooperation of all administrators in education for the fulfilment of their goal and the implementation of their ideas.

On the basis of past experience, the following suggestions can be offered for bringing about qualitative improvement:

1. In the organization of the above institutions, those professionally skilled individuals should be appointed who can understand the problems of school education, seek solutions to them and guide the teachers.
2. At the national level, too, there should be an ideal institution capable of working for the improvement

of education. At present, the NCERT is performing this function, but it is necessary to make its efforts more fruitful in a shorter time frame.

3. So far, universities have remained completely cut off from schools. Now, they should offer their cooperation for the improvement of school education through research, improved curricula, search for new and better methods of teaching and evaluation, teacher training, preparation of superior text-books, etc.
4. In the states, too, there is the need to establish such institutions as—state secondary education board, teacher training board, text-books improvement centre, curriculum research institute, vocational guidance institute, etc.
5. At the district level, there should be strong organization under the direction for the district education officer, and the principals of all training colleges in the district should offer him their cooperation.

The following points should be kept in view in order to make the working of institutions more effective:

(a) In these institutions, only the most capable and highly qualified officials should be appointed, with suitable attractive scales of pay.

(b) These institutions should coordinate and harmonize their activities with each other. For example, the NCERT should associate itself with the state educational institution, departments of universities and district level organizations while district level organization should devote itself to the assistance and supervision of schools, teachers and school organizations.

(c) The functioning of these institutions should be regarded as an inalienable part of the working of the ministry of education and department of education.

If a system of the kind outlined above is introduced, there is little reason to doubt that classroom teaching and research level activities of the highest order will be linked with each other in a single chain. All the problems of education will be tackled as soon as they arise, and new and superior programmes will be formulated and implemented promptly.

System at Work. The fourth programme for the improvement in administration is the modification and modernization of the department's method of working, which, at present, is in a deplorable state. For this purpose, the measures outlined below should be adopted:

1. The department of education in each state should have a wing for the study of organization and working, and it should offer its suggestions for administrative reforms from time to time.
2. In the annual conferences of educational administrators of various levels, information about departmental policies and programmes should be given but addition, they should also be made aware of the change introduced. Their views on these changes should be invited and discussions initiated.
3. The National College, whose establishment has been recommended by the Kothari Commission, should provide opportunities for research into educational administration. In addition it should study the following subjects and offer its suggestions-rules pertaining to admission to educational institutions of particular classes, provision of financial grants to institutions, selection of teachers, evaluation of teaching work, determining the internal and external

techniques of evaluation, adoption of a convenient method for payment of teachers salaries, preparation of text-books and their acceptance, and analysis of the work of official concerned with inspection and supervision.

4. Excessive and unnecessary staff should not be appointed, but at the same time, care should be taken to see that important officials do not waste their time and energies in routine and minor works.

5. Delays in work and inconveniences are occasioned by an irrational division of authority. Hence, as far as possible, more and more administrative and financial responsibility should be shifted to district level officials. The directorate of education should concern itself mainly with coordinating their efforts, formulating policies, and ascertaining whether the authority delegated to them is being properly utilized or not.

In this context, it is to be noted that improvements in departmental working require officials with open minds and hearts. When the organization suggested above it introduced, it is hoped that these administrators will be able to develop the right attitudes.

Salient Features

The fifth step towards the improvement in administration lies in introducing flexibility and dynamism in administration. The problems of India's education are very complex, and the diversities and variety in the country's economic and social conditions have obviated the possibility of finding a single solution for them all, under all conditions. Even this diversity can be converted into a virtue if the method of working is dynamic and flexible. What will happen in such a situation is that varied experiments will be carried out in different situations and contexts, and with their help, solutions will be found quickly and inexpensively. This important principle can best be illustrated through some examples:

1. Under the present educational system, all the colleges and schools in the state have a common curriculum, and whatever changes are introduced usually produce destructive results in certain plans. The reason for this is that those who formulate the curriculum invariably keep their vision fixed upon the weaker and backward students. In consequence, the brilliant students and enthusiastic institutions are never benefited. Besides, the rigid curriculum makes it impossible to exploit the institutional advantages that some institutions may have over others. Hence, it is essential that, in a state, more than one, or at least two curricula—one generalist and the other specialized, must be introduced.

2. The second rigid constraint in the existing system is that the child makes his choice of subjects in class 9, at the age of 14, and then remain tied to this choice for the future. This kind of responsibility, thrust upon the immature child, is as harmful in the long run as th institution of child marriage proved to be. Besides, deciding upon groups of subjects is also counterproductive. In this context, we should be more liberal and the student should be given more freedom in his choice of subjects.

3. No less important is flexibility and variability in the methods of teaching and evaluation. The existing fixed methods, a fixed curriculum and a definite system of education may satisfy the average teacher and the average student. But teachers with creative minds, if prevented from working outside the guidelines fixed by the department, will be completely stultified.

4. Efforts at making secondary education development-oriented and reducing the enrolment in research at the university level have both failed. Hence, a plan should be prepared in which the curriculà for the first degree synthesizes a number of vocational studies. Later on specialized education in those vocations should be provided, to the extent of allowing the candidate to obtain his Ph.D. degree in the subject, if he so wishes.

5. There should be a practical and flexible approach towards the medium of education. So long as regional languages remain incapable of shouldering the burden English should be retained as the medium of education in order to maintain standards.

6. There should be flexibility even in the sphere of education. At present, an excessive expansion in secondary and higher secondary education in certain regions has led to increased unemployment while on the other hand in some regions, these levels of education have been introduced quite recently. In the future, expansion of education should be limited only to the underdeveloped regions only. Besides, tl10se subjects should be encouraged for study, which have remained neglected so far.

7. The current fashion is to give financial grants upon certain fixed principles to all educational institutions with the result that the superior as well as the inferior institution obtain under the same rules and conditions, this policy of uniformity should be modified so as to make provisions for additional grants to the better and more progressive institutions.

It is of course true that it is as difficult and problematic to implement a flexible and dynamic method of education as it is easy and convenient to implement a rigid and uniform system of education. But, in modern society, we just cannot make progress without a flexible and dynamic system. In fact, we must now grant freedom to every student, every teacher and every institution. This is a difficult task, but it is not impossible. In order to make it possible two aspects must be strengthened the teacher, and the administrator.

The Assessment

The need for a continuous evaluation of programmes is self-evident. In fact, planning, implementation and evaluation are mutually correlated functions. They help in overcoming the obstacles that arise during implementation. Besides, they also help in finding solutions to the problems that remain. Unfortunately, we have not laid sufficient stress upon evaluation and research, as yet. We suggest that in the next few years, special emphasis should be laid upon evaluation and educational research.

There are three modes of evaluation, which will have to be adopted simultaneously and continuously:

1. One simple form of evaluation is that, in which each teacher, administrative official of the department and educational institution will have to become involved. In the context of school planning and implementation, the institution should itself periodically evaluate its own progress. Similarly, teachers and administrators should also evaluate their own work. The state as well as the central governments should also evaluate their programmes from time to time to discover whether their policies are being promptly, effective and economically implemented or not.
2. There is need for the evaluation of the programmes and schemes adopted by district level organizations, central government and the state governments.

Realistically, periodical evaluation should be necessarily provided for in every important programme. This provision should provide a clear statement of the aims of evaluation, its process, agency and period. Briefly stated, just as teaching and evaluation are inseparably related, in the same way policy formulation and evaluation should also be regarded as inseparable.

3. There are certain aspects of planning which must be evaluated at the highest level. For instance, there is the very important question how does education contribute to national development, or what contribution can it make? Equally important are the questions of the use of manpower, the need for it, and the opportunities for planning its utilization. In addition, there is the problem of standards in education. In connection with brilliant students at the various levels of education as well as in different kinds of institutions, it is necessary to discover the extent to which they achieve the desired standard. It should be the duty of the Ministry of Education and the Planning Commission to encourage research into this aspect. Famous departments of universities can be beneficially associated with these programmes of evaluation.

Higher Education

The administrative problem of universities are no less complex neither are they in any less need of attention. In this connection, the recommendations and suggestions of the Education Commission should be implemented. We suggest that the Indian branch of the Asian Institute of Educational Planning and Administration, with the cooperation of the University Grants Commission, should take into its hands the work of research into this aspect, and also prepare programmes for the proper, training at the university level. It is also our suggestion that the Planning Commission should establish a working group, under the guidance of the Asian Institute, for a detailed study of these problems, and on the basis of its findings, it should also promptly take definite and concrete steps for the improvement of university administration.

This tendency of spending less and less on educational administration has continued over the years, and in the last three, plan periods, it has become even more marked. In the states' plans, no money is at all allocated for administration and inspection in the first place, and even when some provisions are made, deductions are made in it, whenever there is any need to reduce expenditure. The outcome of this short-sighted policy is that although a small amount of administrative expenditure is saved, a much larger sum is wasted on education because of the lack of proper administration, and inspection.

It is most saddling to note that there is very little awareness of the great, harm that has been caused to educational administration. In many matters, the quality of administration has deteriorated sharply, while in many others, administration has completely vanished. For instance:

1. The director of education is usually so completely occupied by his work in the office that he is unable to undertake regular tours of schools, as he did in the past. He is also unable to establish close relationships with district officials, and thus, he is unable to stimulate or direct them fruitfully. Regional officials also suffer from similar handicaps.

2. The result is that even district officials are often unable to inspect schools for long stretches of time.

3. Many very important responsibilities have been thrust upon the departments of education, but they have failed to evolve an efficient machinery for

implementing their schemes. For instance, text-books have been nationalized, but there is no efficient machinery to oversee the production of text-books of the desired quality or standard. Consequently, in some places, the district inspector has been converted into a mere bookseller, while at other places, he wastes two-thirds of his time in paying the salaries of teachers.

Not only is it necessary to reverse this flow, it is essential to achieve this promptly. Hence, it is suggested that, for the purpose of improving and strengthening educational administration, 5 per cent of the educational budget should be earmarked, on a priority basis, for educational planning, administration and evaluation, and this should also include research and the training of educational administrators, principals, as well as the in-service training of teachers.

The Suggestions

1. Well coordinated and harmonized plans should be framed at the district, state and national levels in order to meet the need for a decentralized approach to educational planning.
2. Instead of allocating funds for a few selected schemes, complete educational plans should be formulated.
3. Institutional plans will provide the basis for this novel process of educational planning.
4. State plans must be made the basis of the entire process of educational planning.
5. The district should be regarded as the basic unit of educational planning, administration and development. From the very next year, district plans should be initiated for purposes of guidance, and these should be adopted within a five-year period.

6. It is the responsibility of the Central Government to adopt and maintain a balanced viewpoint and foresight regarding education development as well as the eradication of regional imbalances among states in the matter of education. From this viewpoint, specific programmes should be included in the national plan. Planning should have a dual aspect-planning from above, and planning from below.

7. It is necessary to involve teachers, intimately and effectively in the formulation and implementation of educational planning.

8. In preparing plans for educational development, the technique of preparing projects should be adopted.

9. The tendency towards heavy investments and negligence of costs in educational development programmes should be curbed; instead, programmes more in keeping with the conditions of a developing country should be prepared.

10. Priorities at the district, state and national level should be clearly defined for effective educational planning.

11. All individuals concerned with educational planning and implementation should be given suitable training.

12. For improvement in the implementation of educational plans, it is essential that the existing organizational administration should be immediately replaced by developmental administration.

13. There is an acute need to establish coordination and harmony between the various agencies concerned with educational planning. The states and the centre, too, should coordinate and harmonize their activities in plan formulation and implementation.

14. Under the new concept of developmental administration, there will be great need for re-organization in the state and central educational services.

15. Programmes for the in-service training of educational administrators should be given a high priority.

16. There is need to encourage departmental officials to increase their professional competence.

17. Giving the highest priority to the Education Commission's suggestion for the establishment of a national college for training such administrators, we recommend that this should be established immediately and developed fully within the five-year plan period.

18. In addition to developing programmes for in-service training, it is also necessary to adopt a programme to complement such training. In this, the administrative officials at every level should be acquainted with the complex problems of educational reorganization.

19. Effort must be made for providing better supervision and guidance to schools.; For this, wherever necessary, the staff for inspection must be increased and subject-inspectors appointed.

20. Departmental working, which is unsuitable for developmental administrafion must be improved quickly.

21. If educational administration is to be improved, proper provisions of institutions and able individuals for the supervision of programmes for qualitative Improvement must be made. These should include the NCERT at the national level, state educational

institutes at the state level, and other institutions and school complexes at the district level.

22. The mode of working of departments of education should be dynamic and flexible.

23. In the forthcoming years, due emphasis should be placed upon evaluation and educational research. In these fields, some determined progress must be made.

24. Priority must be given in the present plan to schemes for reforms in educational planning, administration and evaluation. For this, 5 per cent of the expenditure on education should be set apart for this purpose.

6

School Building and Arrangements

School building is an integral part of learning environment and is of tremendous importance in education. A good school building has a stimulating influence on children; a bad building depresses them. By a good school building we mean a building, simple and beautiful in design, attractive decoration, comfortable seating arrangements, useful service facilities such as libraries, subject rooms, well-equipped laboratories, functional playgrounds, classrooms with chalk boards, sinks, work areas, filing and storage facilities, pupil lockers. Bad school buildings are those which are non-functional, meagerly equipped, and unattractive and unhealthy. The following are the characteristics of a good school building.

(1) Beautiful Healthy Refreshing Place. A good school building has an ideal site. A healthy, beautiful and refreshing environment which soothes the eye, and refreshes the soul can be obtained in an ideal site. The building should be constructed in the outside of the town area where these is more fresh air and where there is a chance of getting adequate playgrounds near the school. In choosing the site the authorities should note carefully the direction in which the town is expanding. It would be unwise to choose a site at a place which may come in the middle of the town in 10 years time. The site should be little raised and these should be no low lying waterlogged area near at hand. If there are trees on the site so much the better. In case there are no trees, a tree planting programme may be started at once. The school compound should have plenty of trees possibly fruit trees.

(2) Serviceable. A school building should have all the aminities for its children. For example, there should an ample space for mid-day meals, common room, retiring room, library and reading rooms, visitors room, headmasters office, teachers room, workshops and laboratories. A school building should have all the facilities for students and teachers.

(3) Adequate Arrangement for Air and Light. A school building should be airy and well ventilated. Classrooms should have enough, doors and windows, special arrangements for light should be made for science and drawing rooms.

(4) Economical. The school building should be not very costly and a minimum expenditure should be made in its construction at least during the present financial crisis. Theoretical classes may run in the open and for practicals rooms may be got prepared.

(5) Arrangement for Fresh Drinking Water. There should be a proper arrangements for fresh drinking water.

Maintenance of School Building. Some Headmasters and Principal of schools take joy and happiness in achieving educational goals through curriculum development, and cooperative interaction with teachers, parents and community. They relish their work connected with public relations, supervisory activities and staff meetings. And there are others who take pride in managing things rather than people. Their interests are closely related to devising better physical environment for the persons who serve in the schools and for pupils who come there to receive education. The effective school Principal strikes a balance between these two functions:

(*a*) dealing with personnel,

(*b*) improving physical environment.

He not only spends time in discussing matters with the architects and engineers regarding school structure and design, he not only plans the building in consultation with teachers, parents and other members of the community his proposed school will serve, but he supervises construction also because plans on paper may not work out as anticipated.

The Principal being in charge of the building has to look to the maximum utilization and its maintenance also. It is he who can get cooperation of his teachers in maintaining the building in proper condition. He should help his teachers feel that the building is theirs to care for. Whenever he gets a suggestion from his staff for preventive maintenance he should welcome it and try to translate it into action as for as possible. A machinery should be set up to get repairs done immediately they come to his notice. A stitch in time saves nine' applies equally well to the maintenance of school buildings, and their equipment.

Principles for Determining the Building Needs of a School

School Administrators are urged to think of new constructions in terms of the quality of school living to be sought for in years ahead during which a proposed new plant is likely to be in operation.

Before we take a final decision to erect a new school building, a careful survey of the building needs of the whole community should be made. The surveyor should give particular attention to the educational needs of the locality which the contemplated building is expected to serve. The survey should not be made by outsider agencies. It should be made by outsider agencies. It should be required to live his help only when it is considered necessary.

Building Needs of a Counity. In making the survey of the school building needs of a community, attention should be particularly directed to the following:

1. The extent of the use of the present school shall be decided by the school administrator before launching upon the planning of new building. New buildings cannot be justified until the present plant is used to capacity or to near capacity.

2. The number and type of pupil to be immediately accommodated and the number and type to be accommodated within the next 5 years should be ascertained as definitely as possible.

3. The probable building needs for the next 5, 10, 20, 30, years should be calculated and a new building then should be planned and located in relation to this programme. Foresight and forethought are necessary because every school building which is once built has to serve the needs of the community for several years.

4. A schedule of rooms should be prepared far in advance. If, for example, a high school has to be provided for 750 boys in a certain community, a list of rooms required, their uses, size, location in the building, pupil capacity and the location where equipment may be stored, should be drawn out. Such a schedule will guide the architect in making a plan for the building.

Needs of a School Building

A survey made a decade back indicated the dearth of good school buildings in the country. Thousands of schools were found to be housed in unsafe and unusually dirty surrondings, in poorly located buildings, in portable structures, in tents and prefabricated and languishing buildings. A tremendous increase in the student population since the dawn of Independence in the country has been a cause behind this haphazerd construction. There has also been an abrupt increase in birth rate and appreciable rise in construction costs. The rapid increase in school construction in the wake of Independence and nation's concern about free and compulsory education upto 14 within a span of a few years' time also led to this unhappy state of affairs.

Educators should now insist on erecting buildings of simple architectural designs. The programme to be conducted in a school building should determine the design. For example, if a school building is created for elementary schools in rural areas for conducting basic education programme we may have a nucleus type of design for a school with four primary classes to be run in the open.

Considerations for Designing a School Building

If a building for a higher secondary school has to be designed the following considerations should receive our attention.

1. What should be the relation of the individual classroom to the plant as a whole? Classroom is the heart of the educational programme because all activities originate here and are supported. The auditorium or gymnasium cafeteria and other special rooms *e.g.*, art, music, craft or science room are simply accompaniments to the classroom. A school has to be built around the classroom.

2. What should determine the architecture of the school building? Perhaps it is the philosophy of education which determines the nature of the architectural design for a school building. If the nation wants to achieve universal literacy to protect the present democratic setup, classrooms may be designed only

to develop reading, writing, comperhending skills for which they should be simple, adequately spacious, and equipped with comfortable desks. If however, the educational philosophy of the state is such that teachers have to give emphasis on a programme of varied activities classrooms will have to be designed to encourage those activities. If we want that children should develop democratic skills and creative thinking that comes through group discussions. We will have to design the classroom in such a way as to provide enough space for discussion and the furniture will have to be kept moving. If again, a state inculcates in the education progromme work experience for each class, creative expression through arts and crafts, aesthetic experiences, art appreciation, then the classroom will have to be designed in a quite different manner. We will have to provide equipment and supplies as well as space for storing those supplies, movable tables, display areas, craft materials, cabinets, tool boxes, sinks, and exhibit cases.

3. While designing a classroom or determining its equipment the nature of children and adolescents will have to be kept in view. For example, the height of work counters from the floor in the room shall be determined in accordance with the age and maturation level of students.

4. While designing a school building one will have to recognize the needs of children in reference to the physical and social environments from which they come. For example, if a high school is situated in a rural area and boys have to come from a long distance and hence cannot go some during the recess they will have to be provided with lunch rooms. If most children cannot go home during the lunch hour a good cafeteria or a hot lunch counter becomes a 'must.'

In short, the needs of a school building are determined by:

(*a*) The relation of classrooms to the plant.

(*b*) Educational philosophy of the school.

(*c*) Facilities needed to implement the programme.

(*d*) Nature of children.

(*e*) Needs of children.

Healthful School Conditions

'Heathful school environment in a pre-requisite for effective instruction'. A school is expected to provide a healthy, beautiful and refreshing environment which soothes the eye and enlivens the soul. It is a place where the intellectual forces of teachers and students function at there best. Teachers, like anyone else, enjoy a cheerful, and efficient environment. They want pleasant classrooms and comfortable reliting places where they can relax in vacant periods.

The functional efficiency of a school building depends upon its sanitary condition and healthful structure. The following things should be kept in view when planning and erecting a building, so that it may present a healthy environment.

1. Site.

2. Adequate supply of drinking water.

3. Class lavatories.

4. Amenities for students and teachers.

5. Airy and well-ventilated classrooms.

6. Playground.

A school cannot be put up everywhere and anywhere. The site of the school determines what type of school it would become in future. The site should be free from din and dust of busy roads, free from the malodours coming out of brick kilns, free from the smoke ejected by factories and mills. It should have natural drainage and there should be no chance of its being flooded by running water during the rains. It should be far away from dangerous bodies of water, highways with heavy traffic, stone quarries, clift's, forests and dangerous river or canal banks.

The site should not be too far from the area which the proposed school would serve. It should be within easy and feasible distance of pupils who would like to seek admission there. Elementary school children are not expected to walk more than three quarters of a mile and the High School students may walk as much as one mile and a half in coming to their school. Hence, a school site should not be at a greater distance than one to one-and-a half mile from their homes.

The soil of the school site should be sandy loam free from decaying organic matter and also free from debris and dumped material. It should have sufficient underground water supply. The underground water should be of good quality so that water pumps may be provided at different places in the premises. An adequate supply of pure drinking water should be made available inside the school. Water contamination should be guarded against.

One lavatory for every 100 students should be provided within school boundaries. In the absence of proper lavatory arrangements the school building becomes dirty. The atmosphere becomes polluted and the health of pupils suffers. The lavatories and urinals should be washed daily and kept clean. Phenyl should be sprinkled as many times as possible during the school day.

Amenities for students and teachers help in bettering the level of school performance. Some of the amenities which a school should provide are:

1. Separate common rooms for boys and girls.
2. A common resting room for teachers.
3. A visitors' room where parents and visitors may wait.
4. A headmaster's office and an office for clerks.
5. Workshps of standard sizes suitable for the number and needs of children.
6. Latrines, urinals and lavatories accessible from all parts of the school.

Other conditions for making school environment pleasant are:

(a) Providing deal lighting arrangement and proper ventilation in the classroom.

(b) Making equipment ideal.

(c) Making the seating arrangement ideal.

(d) Providing good playgrounds.

Ideal Lighting Arrangement in a Classroom

The destiny of India is now being shaped in classrooms and if the classrooms are lighted and airy, if they are functionally equipped to encourage the future builders of the nation, to develop educationally significant and stimulating programmes, the above statement will be no mere rhetoric but assume an aura of reality and truthfulness.

There are certain set standards as regards lighting and ventilation of a classroom. Lighted area is generally fixed in terms of the floor area. If the standard floor area of a room is 616 square feet for a room of dimensions 22′ × 28′, the normal light area should be 90 to 120 square feet. The classroom should remain flooded with sunlight throughout the school day. The light can come through windows in the walls or through doors. Normally, two doors should be provided, one of which opening into the corridor the main passage in larger school buildings, into which many rooms open. The height of the windows should be such that the amount of light falling on the pupil's desk is adequate. The normal height of a window sill is three feet. But where we have a shortage of desks and students have to be seated on floor or where squatting arrangements have to be made due to one reason or the other, the height of window sills should be not more than 2 feet.

The whole room should be flood-lit either through sunshine or through copious artificial light projected from many directions, eliminating all shadows in surface illuminated. Light in no case should fall on pupils' eyes. Normally it should come from the left, but where it is not possible to so construct the windows in the was and light has to enter the room from the right, it may be tolerated. Seating arrangement may be adjusted in such a way that a full advantage of light coming from the left is derived.

The colour of the classroom walls should be pleasant so as not to jar on pupils' eyes. The ceiling should reflect light shade of ivory. When artificial light arrangements are made there should be adequate and flexible lighting with photo-electric switches and manual controls.

Artificial light is necessary for all rooms in a school which runs in the evening shift. In the winter the sum sets at about 5 P.M. and the school has to run upto 6.15 P.M. It means that children have to read for more than an hour in the artificial light in second shiftad schools. When artificial light has to be installed in classrooms, the fixtures should be of the semi-direct, semi-indirect or indirect type. The most recent plan for ensuring proper illumination is to install a photo-electric cell which automatically turns on the lights when natural illumination falls below a certain designated candle-power. When the natural illumination reaches sufficient intensity the photo-electric cell automatically switches off the light.

Sometimes we have glare on the chalk board which causes discomfort to the teacher and the pupil. Glare can be avoided by having judicious use of window shades. The direct rays of the sun should be prevented from falling on the pupil's eye.

Ideal Ventilation of a Classroom

Ventilation of a classroom is closely related to students-teacher comfort and instructional efficiency. The ideal standard for circulation of air in school buildings is 30 cubic feet of fresh air per minute per pupil. But such a great movement of air is unnecessary. School-room ventilation has to do not only with air movement, but also with humidity and temperature. The movement of air is closely related to humidity and temperature.

Cross-ventilation is a simple and a very economic device for proper air movement through the room. In rich and advanced countries air movement is provided in two ways: gravity system and forced ventilation.

Ideal Equipment of a Classroom

The following are suggested as desirable attributes of a generously equipped classroom in which a full and varied educational programme can be carried out. But it should be remembered that it is unwise to provide elaborate resources which may lie unused because they are not needed.

1. Classroom area—a minimum floor area of 616 square feet and a minimum light area of 100 square feet.

2. Chalkboard or tackboard, portable or slideboards, nearly 20 linear feet.

3. Storage space—cubicles for children, shelves for books, filing cabinets.
4. Furniture—a variety of single desks, round and square tables of varying heights.
5. Toilet facilities—preferably attached to a classroom.
6. Easy access to auditorium or gymnasium.
7. Floor covering which may tend to reduce noise.
8. Two exits from the classroom—one leading to the corridor, the other leading directly outdoors.
9. Shades, draperies and venetian blinds for darkening room for use of audio-visual materials.
10. Workspace in corner or end of the room with sink and work shelves.

An ideal classroom has the following qualities:

1. It is a light, clean, and easy-to-care-for room.
2. It lends itself to a variety of purposes and uses.
3. It lends itself to a programme for children of a given age range.
4. It provides an environment which is attractive for both children and teachers with plenty of colour tastefully used.
5. It economises space.

Ideal Seating Arrangement in a Classroom

The school's physical environment should take into consideration the age and maturation level of children it houses. As far as our experience goes, most schools in the country are providing all age groups two kinds of furniture:

1. Single desks with attached chairs.
2. Larger tables with attached or unattached chairs or stools or benches.

The furniture is of a standard size for all pupils of all age groups and of all physical proportions. In every age group the bodily proportions of pupils differ from individual to individual. At every maturation level we have a similar difference. It means that the nature of furniture should be different for different age groups. The size of furniture, the height of the desk or table should suit the height of the child who uses it.

It is not also good to have either single desks or dual desks or larger tables for all children reading in a higher secondary school. Smaller children, who have a tendency to stick together socially, need dual desks or larger tables to work on, whereas the maturer or older children want to work independently; hence, their working tables or desks should be single or separate. Variety is preferable to uniformity.

Ideal seating arrangement in a classroom is either semi-circular or in a quadrant. It ensures equal distance for all pupils; at the same time individual attention is possible for all pupils.

Ideal School Ground

The following are the criteria for an ideal school ground:

1. It covers at least 5 acres of space. A school needs—*(a)* area for building classrooms with necessary open spaces, *(b)* area for playing field, and *(c)* area for staff quarters.

   The area for playgrounds is determined by the variety of games and sports that the school intends to provide. Volleyball, football and hockey are the most popular games in our country and they require smaller areas of land. The area required for games may be 1½ acre to 2 acres on the condition that community parks and open spaces are available in the school neighbourhood for using them as playing fields. Else, an area of 5 acress hould be aimed at.

Area for building classrooms and staff quarters will depend upon the present and future needs of the school and community. If there is a chance of development of habitation, and increase of student population in near future the planners should not be confined to immediate needs. However, 8 to 12 square feet of floor area and 8 to 12 cubic feet of volume is needed for each student; so the space for building classrooms will be calculated on the basis of area required for one classroom. In general, at least 600 to 900 square feet are needed for a classroom. A hall and library and laboratories need nearly triple the floor area.

2. It should be safe and healthful.
3. It should be free from traffic hazards.
4. The school ground should be free from undue noise.
5. It should be free from disagreeable odours.
6. It should be well drained and free of erosion.
7. It should have play areas for different age groups.
8. It should include some hard-surfaced play areas.
9. It should be attractively landscaped.
10. It should be kept clean and attractive.
11. It should include garden plots.

❋❋❋

7

Position of Headmaster

The Headmaster of a school is not only a professional man but he is a professional leader too, because he inspires, guides, directs and manages the whole educative process. He sets the pattern and guides the outcomes of a cooperative action. He generates enthusiasm for a project and inspires work towards its solution.

He is not a boss but a leader. The boss drives his men: the leader coaxes them. The boss depends on authority the leader depends on goodwill of his associates. The boss creates fear in his people the leader inspires them. The boss assigns the task: the leader sets the pace. The old concept of bossism in educational leadership is now fast dying out.

The Headmaster of a school in a democratic setup has to accept and profess democratic values which state that:

(1) Greater efficiency is gained in carrying out of group decisions.

(2) Time is saved when people understand what they are to do.

(3) People will act most wisely when they are carrying out their own decisions.

(4) Facts grow in value and importance in direct proportion to their circulation, etc.

He has a firm belief in what Prof. Humayun Kabir once said, "If our democratic way of life is to survive, it is necessary that our children should grow up using and understanding its techniques." He understands very well that no institution has greater opportunity than the school to make democracy conscious of itself. No school can be the cradle of democracy if the same cradle is rocked by the person who runs it.

He is aware of the underlying principles of democratic leadership, namely, sharing responsibility, equality, freedom, cooperation, justice, recognising individual worth as listed in a previous section. He looks upon his personnel as socially equal to himself; he desires to be known to his staff as a brother rather than their boss. He is not the supreme law-giver who makes all decisions and promulgates them; but he takes decisions with his staff and not by himself. He makes them responsible, divides responsibilities, and shares in administration he runs. The principle of sharing responsibility is the keynote of his policy. He delegates to his senior teachers headship of morning assembly, incharge-ship of students' fund, games and sports, examination and evaluation of students because he realizes their worth. He is the chairman of games, the President of the Parent-Teacher Association, the head of the literary society, but he never desires to be at the top.

To him the school is a cooperative society which has to be run on sound principles of cooperation. The democratic setup of the school management requires cooperative interaction within the school community which is composed of teachers, other employees, students and parents. It is vital in the interests of the school at a democratic institution that the leader should permit all the persons concerned and affected by decisions share in the process of shaping them. He makes a deliberate effort to use this interaction in reaching the best possible decisions.

When the school staff thinks and plans together in an atmosphere of mutual trust, confidence and respect, the best thinking of all influences group behaviour and shapes wholesome decisions. When the group applies wholehearted cooperation to the solution of school problems, there is a much greater chance of arriving at the right solutions. When every member feels that his ideas are sought, welcomed and respected by his Head the group morale becomes strengthened. There is greater support for executing policies which are a result of cooperative deliberation because the group thinks that these are our policies rather than those of the Headmaster's. As the staff has shared in reaching decisions, they are expected to abide by them. Hence, there is greater initiative and sympathy in carrying them out. Teachers can interpret most intelligently to parents these practices or policies which they have helped the Headmaster to shape.

Such are the values of a democratic leadership of a school.

Qualites of a Democratic Educational Leader

The qualities which the Headmaster as a democratic professional leader should possess, emerge from what has been discussed above.

These qualities are listed below:

1. Ability to delegate powers and duties.
2. Ability to stimulate and encourage growth .among staff members.
3. Ability to co-ordinate the efforts of the school community.
4. Ability to direct the implementation of those policies which the group recognizes as sound and practicable.
5. Ability to organize teaching staff so that there is freedom for and encouragement to creative contribution to instructional improvement.

6. Ability to improve the morale of co-workers by praising them when they have done good work for the school.
7. Ability to keep the associates working as individuals, as wen as, as a group with a common objective and a common goal.
8. Ability to practice democracy in school management by cooperatively determining school aims and procedures with teachers. pupils and their guardians.

These are some of the qualities which the democratic professional leader of an educational institution should possess. To quote Shane and Yauch, "Creative Educational Leadership is substantially more than the efficient administrative-supervisory execution of Education-Department and school policies. It is a group function and a group process in effective school-policy-making in which the administrative ifficials participate, but in which they do not control or predetermine outcomes."

The Headmaster, as a creative educational leader has a belief as we said earlier, in the importance of group process, cooperative group decisions, and group action.

Extent to which Democratic Leadership has been Achieved in India. The headmaster in most of the schools is expected to keep the school running. He is required to see that the teachers teach and boys learn. There is no genuine professsional leadership in evidence as should be exercised in a democracy. Administrative responsibilities are generally dictated by educational departments and management of school. A number of routine tasks confront him and consume most of his time and energy. He has a number of duties and responsibilities to the public, the management, the teachers, the pupils and the department. Advisory role is played by the Inspector or Education Officer. Responsibility for no aspect of education, *i.e.*, curriculum construction, teaching methods, school policies and procedures is delegated to the Headmaster or his staff.

Duties and Responsibilities of Principals or Headmasters

The duties, power and responsibilities of the Principal or head of a school are given below. These duties are listed under four heads; administrative, supervisory, organizational and teaching. Bray leaves aside Headmaster's Administrative functions and regards his principal duties as organizational, supervisory and teaching. But in our opinion, the Headmaster is an Administrator first and the last.

Administrative Duties

1. To function as the Head of office and carry out all administrative duties required of a head of office.
2. To be responsible for the proper maintenance of accounts and schools records, service books of teachers, other registers, returns and statistics as are prescribed by the Department.
3. To ensure that the school gets full complement of teaching staff, furniture, science equipment, library books and other teaching aids and towards that end to send his requirments for these to the department.
4. To submit official correspondence relating to school and furnish all information required by the Inspector of Schools or by the department.
5. To make purchases of stores, etc. required for his school in accordance with the prescribed rules, to enter all such stores in stock register, to scrutinize bills and make payment.
6. To ensure that tuition fees, where levied, are realized and credited to the Government revenues in time.

7. To make all payments in time and according to rules.
8. To grant fee concessions to poor deserving students and to those belonging to scheduled castes, scheduled tribes and backward communities.
9. To conduct physical verification of school property and stocks at least once a year and to maintain the stock registers neatly and accurately.
10. To be responsible for proper utilisation of the Pupils' Funds.

Supervisory Duties

1. To supervise, guide and control the work of the teaching and non-teaching staff of the school.
2. To plan year's work in advance in consultation with his colleagues and to hold staff meetings at least once a month to review the work done during the month and to assess the progress of the pupils.
3. To promote initiative of the teachers for self-improvement and encourage them to undertake experiments which are educationally sound.
4. To help and guide tlte teachers and promote their professional growth and towards this end actively encourage their participation in courses designed for inservice education.
5. To supervise classroom teaching and secure cooperation and coordination amongst teachers of the same subject.
6. To provide special help and guidance to teachers newly entering the profession on their first appoir.tment.
7. To attend to student welfare inside and outside the classroom.

8. To organize teachers for studying curriculum and syllabi in use with a view to analysing the objectives of teaching of the various topics and adapting the instructional programme to them.

Supervision of Classroom Teaching

Supervision of teaching in the Headmaster's first responsibility. He is the teacher of teachers. He encourages his teachers to discover for themselves better way of teaching. He inspires them to experiment with their own ideas. His supervision is not that of corrective type but it is creative. He never says, 'I told you to do this: so do this'. But he often says, "Let us see how your ideal work". He gives friendly advice and not order. He is a friend philosopher and guide. He does not find faults in the teaching. His inspection is never taken as a fright. He judge the effective new of the lesson keeping in view the level of the class, the visual aid used, and the limitation of the teacher. If he differs from the teacher he has conference with him in his office and gives his suggestion there.

So far as student welfare is concerned, he is responsible not only for their physical welfare through systematic medical inspection but he is also responsible for the conduct of his students. If a student is found loading outside while the class is going on who is responsible? It is ineffective control and supervision that makes boys truant and indisciplined. The Principal is responsible for not only supervision of teaching or student welfare, he is responsible for the improvement of every phase of the educational programme.

Supervision of School Records

Much of the time of the Principal is wasted in supervising school records so that they may be properly maintained.

(1) Checking of Cash Books. The principal is personally responsible for proper maintenance of cash books. The cash books are written by some assistants in the office but they have to be daily checked by the Principal/Headmaster so that balances are struck off daily. Other financial documents which the Principal has to supervise are, Fee Registers, Contingent Registers, Acquittance Rolls, Scholarship Registers, Provident Fund Registers.

(2) Checking Examination Register and Progress Report Cards. The Principal/Headmaster has to sign the examination registers and progress report cards and is held responsible for any wrong entry. Other reports which the Principal/ Headmaster has to check carefully are admission and withdrawal registers.

(3) Checking Teachers Diaries. He has to see that his teachers plan their lessons in advance and take classes according to the time table set by him. Hence, he has to check their diaries every week.

(4) Attending Correspondence with the Inspectorate. He has to attend to correspondence with the State Government, Education Department, guardian and other people.

(5) Checking Stock Registers. Stocks are purchased and entered in relevant stock registers—consumable and non-consumable. He has to initial every entry in the stock registers and verify that stocks purchased are in good condition.

Organizational Duties

1. To admit boys, prepare time table, allocate duties to teachers, decide teaching load.
2. To prescribe a regular time table for home assignment.
3. To evaluate students' progress, and send progress reports regularly.
4. To organize special instruction to boys and girls who are either very weak or gifted.

5. To organize periodically educational excursions after proper planning.

6. To develop and organize library resources and reading room facilities.

7. To organize and coordinate cocurricular activities.

8. To promote the physical well-being of the students, secure high standards of cleanliness and health habits and arrange periodical medical inspection and take follow-up action.

The organizational responsibilities of the Head of a school include provision of inside and outside school activities. These activities are physical, social, cultural and intellectual—all organized in a balanced way.

Teaching Functions. The Principal or Headmaster, in many states of the country, is required to take at least 12 periods per week. It means that he is expected to teach 2 periods per day. He is not only to supervise teachers, work, but to give model lesson to students, preferably of the lower class in the school. The Headmaster more than any other member of the teaching staff has to keep himself. In close contact with the developments in educational methods, psychology, physiology and hygiene. Otherwise, how can he guide his teachers well?

Duties of Public Liaison. He has to act as Public relations officers. He has to maintain healthy elations with the teachers, pupils, guardians and the community at large. His relations with his assistants are at ways happy. A good Headmaster' says K.G. Saiyidain is one who can inspire his colleagues without dominating over them like a hard task master. He keeps a personal contact with every pupil. He is sympathetic towards them, listens to their difficulties and solves their problem a promptly.

He maintains a liaison with the public, and guardians, seeks their cooperation invites them to discuss various problems connected with the wetfare of students and the school.

He works in conformity with the ideals of the community in which the school in situated. He keeps healthy relations with the country at large. He tries io bring the community in his school and take his school into the community.

Position of Headmaster in a School

The position of the Headmaster in a school can be compared to the position of a captain in a ship. The captain leads the ship, the Headmaster leads the school. It means that he is a leader—a person who conducts others, by going in front of them, a person who directs movement of others, a person who guides actions and opinions and sets the ball rolling. As a leader the main functions of the Headmaster are:

1. Stimulating Teachers. The ability to encourage and aid teachers to work creatively is probably the most important function of the Headmaster. He motivates professional growth through a good school climate which creates by making every teacher realize that his work is important and he is important, by giving, credit when due, by letting him know in advance about changes that will affect him by treating him as an individual, and not as a member on the payroll. He makes the climate of the school good by fostering security and satisfaction, promoting feelings of achievement, economic security freedom from fear, love and affection, self-respect and sharing. He creates group morale by inviting all the members of the staff to share in making plans, in determining the procedures to be used, and in having some chance to determine the efficacy of the results. Teachers work best under such a climate, achieve maximum growth and satisfaction. Growth on the job implies that the teacher recognises that he is personally and professionally progressing.

The Headmaster creates a good climate for the learner also. He organizes learning in such a way that the learner is aware of the progress he is making. That the Headmaster does through a programme of continuous appraisal and evaluation. When the learner knows the progress at the time it occurs, he progresses in achievement.

2. Guiding Teachers. The Headmaster, guides his teachers When teachers request conferences with him he participate in them; he takes an active part in classroom group work, *e.g.*, in the science laboratory if he is interested in science. He coordinates the teachers' activities. He gives guidance for teachers' professional growth. Like a consultant he assists teachers in selecting and organizing subject matter, in preparing outlines for teaching to do the class. He studies the changes in the behaviour of children through a continuous process of evaluation and guides his teacher in the work. Like a true guide he helps them to attain the goals of the school. He uses teachers to help each other. When colleagues cooperate in helping each other to improve in teaching, the quality or claasroom becomes better.

3. Directing Teachers' Actions. The Headmaster directs actions of his teachers. He is concerned with improving teaching; so he visits classrooms, meets teachers individually and in groups, directs teaching, arranges demonstrations. He presides at staff meetings, suggests what his teachers should read, and offers criticism of teaching. He gets tests prepared and measures pupils' progress. He uses and directs the use of diagnosis and guidance services.

In order that he may guide his men well, he has a great-ability to discharge his responsibilities listed below:

1. Responsibility to children whom the school serves.
2. Responsibility to know the basic patterns of development of children.

3. Responsibility to dssume leadership in professional discussions.

4. Responsibility to understand teachers as individual being and the factors that motivate their behaviour.

5. Responsibility to coordinate activities of all members of the staff.

6. Responsibility to guide research activities.

7. Responsibility to set an example to act democratically. Though he is responsible for the efficient functioning of the school, yet he delegates his responsibilities to his teachers.

The Headmaster of a school is a person on which all people depend, whether they are teachers, or students or the parents. He occupies, therefore, a key position in the school. "What the main spring is to the watch, the fly wheel to the machine, or the engine to the steamship," the Headmaster is to the school", says P. Wren. It is the main spring that gives motive power to the clockwork: it is the fly wheel that regulates the machine, it is the steam engine that moves the ship. So it is the Headmaster who inspires and motivates his teachers to achieve goals of the school: it is the Headmaster who regulates the work of the school and brings order in it; it is the Headmaster who runs the school effectively.

As a Headmaster of the school he plays various roles. He is an administrator. He is a supervisor or consultant. He is an organizer of school plant. He is a teacher of teachers: a leader of the community. He is a sociologist who establishes better social relations with all. He is a technical expert in educational measurement and evaluation. He is a skilled worker in group dynamics. He is a liaison officer between the departmental authorities and the public. The Headmaster is not only a leader but an organizer, business director, coordinator, superintendent, friend, philosopher and guide.

As an Administrator. His functions are those of administration, organization, and supervision. School administration means control of school affairs by planning, directing, controlling, executing and evaluating the educative process. School administration aims at progress in learning teaching situation.

As an Organizer. Organization means making arrangements for an undertaking involving cooperation. In this sense school organization involves grouping children, improving classroom structure, reporting students' progress, promotion policies, the use of resources, services and materials of instruction, determining needs of school buildings, providing necessary requisites for effective school instruction, making arrangement for ideal furniture, ideal physical environment, improving the tone of the school by creating a good social climate in the school, building happy and congenial relations with the community, organizing co-curricular activities and coordinating them, maintaining school records ns required by the department, are some or the functions that a Headmaster has to perform in organizing the school.

As a Supervisor. Supervision means helping each other, counselling with each other, planning with each other, or talking with each other about how to improve the teaching-learning situation. It, no more, means directing and judging an activity. It merely means guiding an activity with the supervision which one exercises by virtue of his experience in the field. The supervisor's role is now supporting, assisting and guiding rather than directing. The basic function of the three processes as indicated above—namely, administration, organization and supervision—is the same and it is the improvement of the learning situation.

His qualities of head and heart make him a unique person. His personality is reflected in the school. He is the seal and the school is the wax. He is the hub of the educative process. The success of the school depends upon him. As is the headmaster so is the school. Good Headmasters make good schools. There is cent per cent truth in the saying that the Headmaster is the core stone in the arch of school administration. The functions of the Principal are so varied and complex, so intriguing and numerous that it would take years to acquire the bare knowledge needed to meet the demands of his position. Only a superior intellectual giant can perform them successfully and efficiently.

PERSONALITY OF THE HEADMASTER/PRINCIPAL

The personality of the Headmaster/Principal is reflected in the school administration, organization and supervision. The school is but a lengthened shadow of the Principal, as has often been stated. It is not a mere rhetoric. The great movements in education began with the vision of great Headmasters. The greatest schools, which have carned name and fame have been intertwined with the activities of educational leaders who ran them. The person who directs a department or runs an enterprise makes what it is. A well-qualified head of an institution, school, department or any business enterprise overcomes all difficulties and makes his institution, school, department of business enterprise, function to the highest degree.

"As is the Priest, so is the Parish," says a Russian proverb. The same is true of a school. As is the Principal, so is the School. What General Grant once said about colonels can be remarked about Headmasters. There are no poor regements but poor colonels. So there are no bad schools but bad Headmasters. A splendid school has been ruined by an inefficient headmaster: a wrecked school has been immediately improved by an efficient leader.

It is the personality of the Crown that makes the public what it is. It is something strange and unique in every Headmaster or Principal that attracts peoples towards him and gives confidence to them. It is the confidence that the head has in himself and the confidence he has in his staff that ensure his accomplishments. If he does not have it he fails. The one formula for success as a Headmaster of a school is his personality—a pleasing, attractive personality, pleasing even to the most critical and intelligent man. He has a knack of doing right things at the right time in the right way and, for and by the right people and that is the essense of his successful administration. The efficiency of the school administrator is measured by the extent to which it contributes to teaching and learning. The school administration which does not facilitate education is parasitic and is debauchery of public money. The school administration, which cannot manage the school plant to the best advantage of children and youths of the community it serves, is runious folly.

Signs of an Efficient School Administration

One would like to know what it is that makes administration a success and what are the signs and symptoms of an efficient administrative control. Democracy in administrative procedures, proper use of school plant, judicious use of public funds, broadminded supervision. flexibility are some of the features of successful administration.

***(a)* Democracy.** The effective Principal plans, directs, controls, executes and evaluates the education programme of the school democratically. It is not he alone that does all these functions. It is the cooperative effort of the group—the parents, the teachers and interested members of the community. The guiding principles of his administrative procedures are freedom, flexibility and adaptability. All are given full freedom in planning the educational programme.

Decisions are arrived at by the group as a whole and responsibilities are shared.

***(b)* Control over School Funds.** The control over public funds makes a man fall or rise in the eyes of the public. An honest headmaster uses government and pupils' moneys judiciously and tries to eliminate troubles from the Department and tensions among the staff members and makes use of the public funds for the welfare of student community.

(c) **Proper Use of School Plant.** The efficiency of school administration is judged by the degree to which the school plant is operated and managed. The school plant includes school building and equipment, teaching and non-teaching staff, and students. If the school building is maintained properly, if the right teacher takes the right class at the right time, if cocurricular activities are organized in a fruitful manner, if students are disciplined and their academic achievement is above normal, we say that the school machinery is being effectively used and the administration is good.

An average Principal spends his time and energy in routine office administration, in answering telephone calls, in chatting with casual visitors, in checking up stores. He neglects the personnel programme, the organization, coordination and evaluation of the cocurricular programme, the supervision of instruction. We do not intend to say that he should not see that his office functions efficiently, that he should not attend to telephone calls, that he should not receive visitors, but these are very trivial functions of a good Principal which he can delegate to his assistants also. His main functions are to see that

(i) The cocurricular programme is varied and controlled.

(ii) The school buildings are maintained properly and utilized fully.

(iii) The business duties are handled quickly and accurately.

(iv) The community duties are performed to establish good public relations.

(v) A better instruction is provided to boys and girls through effective supervision.

(vi) The internal administration is effective.

Good Principals make good school and success of the Principal lies in use of intelligence and tact, and preformance of more important duties with faith and vigour.

Problems that a Headmaster Faces

No school can claim to be a No-Problem School and problems crop up daily. There are problems which students create, there are problems which teachers create and there are problems which Principals themselves create. These are problems of human relationships.

There are problems which administration creates. These are administrative and financial problems. These are related to school system imposed by the department over the Principal. For example, when the Education Department requires that your school should run in the evening shift and a girls school in the morning shift, it creates a lot of problems for you. So the problems that a Principal faces may be classified as:

(1) Problems Relating to Teacher. The teaches has now become more right-minded than what he was in 1960's. Lack of interest in teaching work, lack of devotion to duty, resentment against extra work, indiscipline among teachers are some of the ticklish problems that face the Principal/ Headmaster today. But there are solutions to these problems. Senior and more experienced teachers should be entrusted with supervision of the work of the junior and less experienced ones. Special recognition should be given to those who deserve it. Responsibilities should be shared to solve some of these problems. For those teachers who are unsuitable, in-service improvement programmes may be arranged, ways should be suggested in which their purposes may be served better. A continuous inservice work programme may be planned and it should be seen that the concerned tcacher grows in stature. Teachers who are not qualified or whose subjects matter knowledge is poor may be given permission to appear at public examinations to improve their qualifications.

(2) Problems Created by Students. Students present complex and varied problems daily. There are pupils who use obscene talk, pupils who scribble dirty things in the school lavatory, who neglect home work, who use unfair means in the tests, who come late to the school and run away and loaf outside, who play truant, who remove posters, maps and charts, and are troublesome in the assembly, in the classroom or on the playground. These boys are sent by the classroom teachers, the games teacher or the physical education teacher at odd hours, off and on, tt the Principal. The problems created by pupils need urgent and tactful solution.

Here are some suggestions to solve these problems. Most of the student problems arise because of bad relations between the head and pupils or because of strained relations between the teachers and pupils. A psychological understanding of their developmental nature, of their needs and interests may help the school authorities in eliminating some of the undesirable modes of behaviour. A student council or Bal Sabha properly organized gives them a sense of responsibility and is very useful in training them self-discipline which is the true discipline.

(3) Problems Created by Class IV People. Problems relating to class IV servants are not very acute. There is, however, a lack of interest on the part of these servants; for example, the sweeper does not sweep the school premises well, the waterman shirks bis duty, the peon wastes his time in gossip, the chowkidar is found to be away in his duty hours. The Headmaster should build good human relations with this category of employees too. Every attempt should be made to keep them satisfied, and build up morale and good school climate for them. If more class IV servants are needed as the enrolment increases, human relations should not be embittered by saving money.

(4) Problems Created by the Parents. Parents create problems for the school Headmaster when the relations between the two are not good. They criticise school system inordinately sometimes. They can be classified in two groups—the friendly and constructive and the unfriendly and destructive. The latter group is vocal and often influential, out of all proportions to its size. The Headmaster may depend upon the well-meaning and interested parents as his real friends and win over those who are bigoted and biassed. The parent, who rises in wrath against the school for some imagined slight or fancied deficiency in its programme, who makes a community uproar by making a personal crusade against the school, can be dealt with tactfully. Good human relations with all sections of the community, based on sound principles, built over long years may silence the critics. The Headmaster is advised to concentrate on positive building of good public relations rather than engage in mutually destructive counter attacks. He should use different strategies for dealing with the malicious critic, and with the uninformed or professional gossip. If he, through his initiative, makes community an educational partner in the total educational programme of the school, through Parent Teacher Associations, or Parent study circles or Parent Teacher conferences, effective good relations can be built.

(5) Administrative and Financial Problems. The headmaster has much clerical work to do. He has to attend to complex and varied problems of business management. Funds have to be found for extending building facilities, for paying increasing salaries; for purchasing equipment and furniture because his school is becoming bigger due to a larger number of students seeking admission there. In schools of smaller size the responsibility of the total business operation rests solely on the Headmaster and his clerical staff. In bigger schools specially trained persons and qualified upper division clerks have to be employed to take over many of the Headmaster's or Principal's responsibilities related to business management, finance, employment and direction of class IV servants. He has to spend an excessive amount of time on business matters. His skill lies in improving the quality of business administration by using imagination to improve current practices and conditions and devising new procedures so that he may devote more time on the improvement of teaching-learning situation in the school.

(6) Problems of Value Conflicts. The above are very trivial problems which can be solved easily but more difficult problems than these also are confronted by a Headmaster. There is a difficult problem of value conflicts which the Headmaster has to solve. For example, people want an educational programme in which students should be able to reach a standard of minimum academic essentials and at the same time they want that they should become beneficiaries of personal-social development and self-realization in an atmosphere conductive to good mental hygiene or they may require of a school that it should equip children with classical knowledge but have many skills of craftsman: or the public requires that children should be spared from repeating a class except under unusual circumstances, at the same time they say that without promotion for good work or fear of failure neither the gifted nor the slow maturing child will be motivated to study. The Headmaster has to solve such conflicts among and between values. He has to decide whether he should be a democratic or an authoritarian leader. The problem of becoming an authoritarian leader in a democratic setup and a democratic leader in an authoritarian setup presents a dilemma. He has to examine the various competing theories of learning, conflicting philosophies, divergent views regarding child development which are competing for getting his support and has to proceed in the direction in which his intelligence takes him and his beliefs point.

Another dilemma which the Headmaster now faces is authority *vs.* responsibility dilemma. Legally, his is the responsibility for the growth of children and the betterment of the school, but he is asked to share it with his staff. Some able headmasters resolve this dilemma by insisting that the authority and responsibility is theirs alone.

But again there is a difficulty. Democracy does not want things to be done like that. Perhaps a better way would be that though legally he is responsible for seeing that the school operates in the best way, he should choose to invite his teachers to share his responsibilities and help him to determine the nature of his duties, instead of these duties being imposed upon him by the department or the management. In doing so, he should not fear that he will have to apologize to the department or the management or the community for the quality of the school. It is out firm belief that when group decisions are made cooperatively by mature, professionally-minded teachers, they are likely to be superior to those that arise from the Headmaster's single unsupported judgement.

***

8

Role of Teacher and Relationship

The National Commission on School Teachers has described the role of the teacher in the context of the present needs of India as:

> "Today the average teacher's perception of his role and responsibility is far too limited and is concerned with his own immediate tasks, namely the teaching of the 3 R's and later, covering the subject matter prescribed for the examinations. The teacher must actively and feelingly associate himself, as an essential and responsible partner, in the great tasks which face the nation. If the four national goals were to become the actual motive force and the ideals that every man, woman and child in our land would live by, the teacher must intervene in a big way. The formation of character, a character evolved in response to the national goals, would constitute his primary task. He will indeed prepare students for examinations, and open to them the world of knowledge. But these will count for little unless he has helped them become persons of character. There is the personal aspect of character-building to develop qualities like honesty and integrity and there is the social aspect which defines national character. Such a character identification must not be based on cultural and religious traditions of

anyone group but must find acceptance by all sections of the people."

The National Commission on Teachers for Higher Education listed the following roles of teachers in national development:

1. Teacher as an agent of change.
2. Teacher in the context of explosion of knowledge—to remain up-to-date.
3. Teacher to adopt new methodology to utilize interactive methods of instruction.
4. Teacher as a procurer of knowledge to enlarge the sphere of his knowledge.
5. Teacher to use his creative ability.
6. Teacher as an agent of cooperation with community.
7. Teacher to undertake problem-solving research.
8. Teacher to initiate management change.

Different Roles

Parent Surrogate (Parent substitute). A teacher is expected to act as a parent of the students and treat them with affection and care.

Ego-supporter. He is expected to build up and maintain a healthy and strong 'ego' and 'self-concept' among children.

Helper. The teacher is expected to be a helper to students by way of providing them academic and personal guidance.

Resource Person. He is expected to play the role of a resource person who possesses knowledge of the subject-matter and skills better than the students.

Facilitator of Learning. He is expected to promote significant learning among his students.

Limiter or Reducer of Anxiety. He is expected to assist students to control their impulses and reduce anxiety about conduct and performance in different problematic situations.

Detective. He acts as a detective in detecting offences and rule breakers.

Referee. He is expected to settle disputes among students in an objective and fair manner.

Inspirer and Exemplar. He is expected to behave in a manner whereby the traits exemplified by him may be emulated by the students.

Group Leader. He is expected to act as a leader in developing suitable climate and cohesion in the class as a social group.

Judge. He is expected to evaluate the academic and other performance of the students in an impartial manner.

Friend and Philosopher. He is expected to play the role of a friend, philosopher and guide to the students.

Confidant. He is expected to win and share the confidence of the students.

Upholder of the Norms and Values. He is expected to uphold the norms and values of the society.

Moral Educator. He is expected to inculcate the attitudes and moral values cherished by the society among the students.

Democrat. He is expected to play the role of a democrat.

Secularist. He is expected to play the role of a secularist by having an open mind on the beliefs of all religions.

Rationalist. He is expected to play the role of a rationalist by basing his actions on reason.

Initiator. He is expected to play the role of an initiator by exploiting the new technology to the best advantage of the students and the purposes of education. He should play the roles of a planned organizer of curricular innovator of educational ideas, practices. and systems, writer of Radio and T.V. lessons and programmes, user of video-tapes and computers etc.

Equalizer. He should act as equalizer by working for minimizing inequalities in the educative process and by building up an egalitarian, secular and socialist society.

Reformer. In a country like India, where conservatism and superstitions prevail, a teacher is expected to play the role of a social reformer.

Various Responsibilities

(i) Character and personality of the students.

(ii) Classroom management.

(iii) Professional growth and ethics.

(iv) Community relationship.

(v) Total school effectiveness.

Development of Character and Personality of the Students

1. To create an environment of purposeful order, to enlist students assistance in orderly, friendly, courteous and cooperative interpersonal relations.
2. To develop a respect for the rights, privileges, opinions, property and individualities of others.
3. To set a standard of classroom and school environment behaviour which conforms to socially acceptable behaviour.

4. To create group situations which will develop desirable leadership and followers hip qualities in the students.

5. To direct discussion and develop understanding on moral and other ethical issues in order to develop understanding of the reasons for ethical standard.

6. To encourage individuality in each student's thinking and action.

The Teacher and Classroom Management. This implies the creation of an environment in the class as it allows for the best display of the students' abilities in the teaching-learning process. There is the maximum involvement of the students in the classroom activities. The teacher and the students are full of enthusiasm. The classroom environment is based on mutual goodwill and faith. The teacher gives due regard to the individuality of the students and the students in turn show spontaneous respect for their teacher. The teacher in the true sense is the friend, philosopher and guide of the students.

Management of the Class

These roles may be listed as under:

- Communicator of attitude, knowledge, skills and values
- Coordinator
- Curriculum planner and implementer
- Democrat
- Facilitator
- Guide
- Disciplinarian
- Evaluator of attitudes, knowledge and skills

- Helper
- Integrater of knowledge
- Leader
- Improviser
- Innovator
- Motivator
- Observer
- Programmer
- Researcher
- Scientist

Broadly speaking an effective classroom management include:

1. Curriculum Development and Implementation.
2. Adjustment to Individual Differences and Development.
3. Dynamic Techniques of Instruction.
4. Use of Technology of Teaching.
5. Evaluating and Discussing Students' Performance.
6. Maintaining Class Discipline.

Curriculum Development and Implementation. This implies:

1. Determining the object, scope and methods of the grade and subjects to be taught.
2. Participation in grade level or subject matter study of existing curricula and in the development of improved expanded curricula.

3. Devising assignments, when necessary, in order to enrich the teaching programme for the students.

4. Correlating his subject matter curriculum with the curriculum of other subjects.

Adjusting to Individual Differences and Development Levels. This calls for:

1. Drawing upon and applying basic knowledge of the psychology of the child in order to establish readiness for learning.
2. Developing in each student a sense of personal growth and value.
3. Making an effort to know as much as possible about the background and out-of-school environment of each child, in order to improve the teaching learning process.
4. Maintaining discipline by being consistently friendly, fair.
5. Handling behaviour problems in a controlled manner.

Dynamic Techniques of Teaching (Effective teaching learning). This includes:

1. Selecting materials, teaching aids and methods which will facilitate the learning process and stimulate the desire for further learning.

2. Meeting the needs, backgrounds and capacities of the children, being taught.

3. Teaching by use of a suitable variety of lectures, discussions, demonstrations, visual and oral presentations, recitation, directed group effort, experimentation, special projects and field trips.

4. Endeavouring to obtain and maintain student interest and attention so that teaching is done in a receptive atmosphere.

5. Analyzing and evaluating the effectiveness of various teaching techniques in order to improve the learning process.

6. Endeavouring to assure that material taught is applied in such a manner as to develop a pattern of understanding for future use in other areas.

7. Enlisting student participation in the lesson planning process.

8. Developing desirable work and study skills and habits.

9. Developing broad outlines and objectives to be attained within prescribed limits, for a subject or skill area based upon the needs and interests of a specific group of students.

10. Making suitable lesson plans.

Use of Techniques of Teaching. This relates to:

1. Use of blackboard.

2. Use of charts, models, graphs etc.

3. Use of new technology, *i.e.* computer, radio and T.V.

Evaluating and Discussing Student is Performance. This comprises:

1. Interpreting test results and related findings to student progress in order to improve the teaching learning process.

2. Devising and administering appropriate tests to measure the level and quality of student's learning.

3. Discussing student's achievement with the parents individually; in groups and conferences.

4. Reporting student's achievement and progress to parents by means of progress reports.

5. Cooperating and enlisting the cooperation of school specialist in the process of evaluation.

Maintaining Discipline. This implies:

1. Basing discipline on 'do's' rather than 'don'ts'.

2. Showing due regard to the personality of each student.

3. Maintaining a certain reserve but friendly environment.

4. Insisting on good conduct and manners.

5. Displaying sympathetic but firm attitude.

6. Becoming fair and just.

7. Using polished and sweet language.

8. Avoiding threats.

9. Avoiding discussing family problems.

10. Showing humour.

11. Keeping the class busy.

12. Avoiding discussing colleagues.

13. Avoiding sarcastic remarks.

Community Relations

1. To participate in parent-teacher and similar activities.

2. To participate in community affairs.

3. To make himself available to parents at scheduled times to discuss student progress and behaviour.

4. To establish and maintain a good relationship with parents and conducting reporting of student progress, problems and needs.

5. To evince a sympathetic, helpful and understanding attitude towards parents and their children schooling problems.

6. To assure through personal behaviour in the community that the public school staff-image in the community is favourable.

Professional Growth and Ethics

1. To keep abreast of the developments in the teaching profession.

2. To maintain membership in key professional organizations relevant to his subject or area of speciality.

3. To exercise professional discretion in his relations with parents and town's people.

4. To manifest ethical behaviour in his relations with fellow teachers and educational associates.

5. To utilize films, filmstrips, T.V. and radio as a means of keeping abreast of new and advanced knowledge in his field.

6. To keep abreast of subject matter by study of books, periodicals, newspapers and other sources concerning development in his field.

7. To attend conferences, workshops, seminars and meetings; to take field trips which tend to broaden his knowledge.

Total School Effectiveness

1. To accept responsibility for student discipline throughout the school and in the interest of the school as a whole.
2. To execute all required school regulations and assignments on time.
3. To accept his full share of student's activity participation, such as attending athletic contests, etc.
4. To cooperate with all co-workers and to exchange ideas in order to improve and provide variety of approach on the teaching situation.
5. To contribute constructively to committees, faculty meetings and other school system groups.
6. To take the positive steps in developing and maintaining faculty and student morale.

Teacher in Older Days

Modern educators emphasize participative methods. Following are the chief points of difference between a traditional teacher and a participative teacher:

Traditional Teacher	*Participative Teacher*
1. Works on the formulated objectives.	Formulates clearly defined objectives based on the needs of students.
2. Assumes the responsibility	Involves the student's actively in assuming the responsibility of their own learning.
3. Decides what the students need and provides it through lectures etc.	Assists the students to learn to be active information seekers and makes use of all available resources.

Contd.

Traditional Teacher	*Participative Teacher*
4. Focuses on the presentation of content, facts and information.	Focuses on the process of learning learning how to learn.
5. Stresses memorization as a method of learning.	Motivates the students to learn by discovery and exploration, asks questions, formulates problems.
6. Emphasises group performance	Emphasises individual achievement in relation to the student's own needs and objectives.
7. Promotes competition with peers for achievement, recognition, grades and other rewards.	Promotes group work on problem solving activities and learning effectively.

Teacher's Merits

To play their part fully and effectively, the teachers are expected to possess these qualities.

Character and Personality. Character and personality of the students cannot be developed if the teacher who is the model to be followed lacks character and personality. 'Example is better than precept' is an old saying and is absolutely true in the teaching profession. No amount of sermons from the teacher can make much headway. A teacher teaches not only by 'what he says and does' but very largely by 'what he is'. Children are imitative and suggestive by nature. They imitate the dress, voice, habits and manners of their teachers. The likes and dislikes of the teachers become their likes and dislikes. Children who are in the plastic period of their life are easily influenced by their teachers. The teachers should teach what they practise. Gandhiji strongly denounces those teachers who teach one thing with lips and carry another in their heart. Man know thyself is the advice given by Socrates in Greece and Yajnavalkya in India. The teachers must undergo an inner training. They should try to find out their own shortcomings and try to remove them. Ryburn puts it, 'Self-analysis on the part of a teacher is a necessary equipment'. Montessori stresses that every teacher worth his salt must destroy these sins: pride, anger, sloth, sensuality, gluttony and envy. The teacher should be partly a scientist, partly a doctor and completely religious. He must acquire a moral alertness; mingling of patience, love and humility. He should always be frank, sincere and honest. Prof. Raymount urges that the teacher must avoid everything that is petty and mean.

Gandhiji observes, "Woe to the teacher who teaches one thing with the lips and carries another in the heart."

In the words of Dr. Rajendra Prasad, "Their (teacher's) own character should be such that there is no difference between what they say and do. When we act upon this ideal then alone we can be sure of a bright future for our own country."

Arthur B. Moehlmann states, "The teacher and the principal are always on exhibition, observed by hundreds of eyes. The position involves the strain of producing effect upon others not only through the use of specific methodologies, but also through the extension of teacher personality."

The Secondary Education Commission observes, "The teacher has always to realize that all his actions are being watched by his students."

Love for the Profession. The teacher should feel the importance of his profession. He must give his exclusive attention to the growth and development of the personalities of the children under his charge. He would be showing a dishonesty of purpose if once having entered it, he is engaged in other pursuits. Without an exclusive attention to his job he would fail in bringing forth a fine harvest of young men and women who are able to contribute their best for the welfare of mankind. If a teacher takes to his work just to make his living because nothing else is available, he will lack the essential zeal required by the teaching profession. He must be a teacher first and the teacher last. A person who wants to join this profession must feel the call for it. "If a teacher has not an ideal aim, he had better to take to shop-keeping at once, he will there doubtless find an ideal within his capacity:' says Laurie.

In the words of the Secondary Education Commission, "They will not look upon their work as an unpalatable means of earning a scanty living but as an avenue through which they are rendering significant social service as well as finding some measure of selffulfilment and self-expression."

Love for Children. It has been said that if a teacher does not actually like boys and girls, he should give up teaching. He must enjoy their company in groups. A good teacher feels that some sort of energy is constantly supplied by the young. "Love the child and the child will love you; hate the child and the child will hate you:' is a famous maxim. One who does not like children should not stay in teaching.

The Secondary Education Commission remarked, "The good teacher in our reorganized school will endeavour to win the love and confidence of his children and establish his prestige on sincerity, integrity, hard work and a sympathetic handling of their problems."

Respect for the Individuality of the Child. A child should not be treated just like dumb driven cattle. His soul which is pure and very sensitive requires our most delicate care. He has his own individuality. His sense of respect should not be injured. Emerson states, "the secret of education lies in respecting the students." A child wants to be heard and his opinion should not be brushed aside merely because he is a child.

Knowledge of Psychology. Knowledge of psychology goes a long way in providing that basic orientation towards problems of education and child development without which there would be a considerably waste of time, energy and human resources. With a knowledge of child psychology, a teacher will be in a better position to understand and appreciate the individual differences of children, their nature, temperaments, habits and manners.

Intimate Knowledge of the Child. Children are now miniature adults. Their peculiar patterns of thoughts and emotions must be studied. Their names must be learnt and faces recognized. They must not be made to feel that the teacher is indifferent to them. Every source should be tapped to know about them to the fullest possible extent.

Emotional Stability of the Teacher. It is said in The Education and Training of Teacher published by UNESCO, "Various researches show clearly that the emotional stability of teachers affects that of students. Unhappy, frustrated, dissatisfied teachers cannot help their students to become happy, well-adjusted young people." The teachers should try to find out their own shortcomings and try to remove them so that the students may be saved from the adverse influence of their unbalanced personality.

K.G. Saiyidain has observed, "You cannot pour out of a vessel except that you have put into it and, if a teacher is poor and shallow from within, if there is no sparkling wire in him, he cannot quicken the mind or humanize the emotions of his children—if he is not a lighted candle himself, he will never be able to light up the flame in others."

Fully Conscious or the Rights of the Child. A teacher must accept his duty to meet his obligations to the child in the following respects as proclaimed by the International Union of Child Welfare which a federation of national and international organizations to promote the physical, moral and spiritual welfare of the child: *(i)* The child must be protected beyond and above all considerations of race, nationality or creed. *(ii)* The child must be given the means requisite for its normal development-materially, morally and spiritually. *(iii)* The child that is hungry must be fed; the child that is sick must be nursed; the child that is physically handicapped must be helped; the maladjusted child must be educated; the orphan and the waif must be sheltered and succoured. *(iv)* The child must be the first to receive relief in time of distress. *(v)* The child must enjoy the full benefits provided by social welfare and social security schemes, the child must receive a training which will enable it, at the right; time to earn a livelihood and must be protected against every exploitation. *(vi)* The child must be brought up in the consciousness that its talents must be devoted to the service of fellowmen.

Grasp Over the Method. The Secondary Education Commission states, "Any method good or bad links up the teachers and his students into an organic relationship with constant mutual interaction, it reacts not only on the minds of the students but on their entire personality, their standard of work and judgement, their intellectual and emotional equipment, their attitudes and values. Good methods which are psychologically and socially sound may raise the whole quality, bad methods may debase it."

The creative teacher always keeps himself in touch with the latest methods of teaching and uses them in his class. Good methods, which are psychologically sound, facilitate learning and inculcate 'love of work". Two farmers may possess an equal amount of land, an equally great desire for rich harvest but the one who uses the best method of farming will, other things being equal, get better results. Similarly, a teacher who adopts proper methods of teaching will show better results and make his teaching more interesting and effective. A teacher should not be wedded to any particular method and must not have a conservative outlook but use every developed and progressive method in his class as required by the intellectual attainment of the particular students in the particular environment. He ought to devote some of his time in exploring new methods which may be of more help to him.

Mastery of the Subject-matter. A teacher must be a master of his subject. Any weakness on his part will lower his prestige in the eyes of his students. Besides, he must love his subject. A teacher who does not love his subject fails to inspire his students and runs the risk of becoming a hypocrite.

According to the University Education Commission, "No teacher who is not a master of the field, who is not in touch with the latest development in his subject and who does not bring to bear upon his duties a free and untrammeled mind will never succeed in inspiring youth with the love of truth which is the principal object of all higher education."

Daily Preparation. Perhaps there is no type of work where the results of poor planning are so devastating as in teaching. Careful and systematic arrangement of the subject-matter and the classroom activities is conducive to creative discipline. A well prepared lesson helps to overcome the feeling of nervousness and insecurity especially so common in the first attempt at teaching. Bagley emphasises the importance of daily preparation in these words, "However able and experienced the teacher, he could do never without his preliminary preparation."

Democratic Attitude. A teacher cannot afford to be an autocrat. Present day education lays much stress on the inculcation of democratic ideals in the students. A teacher who is to show the way of democracy to the students must develop in himself a democratic attitude. His role is of a friend, philosopher and guide and not of a policeman.

Skill in Questioning. The success of a class teacher in the class also depends on the art of questioning. One who questions faultlessly, teaches effectively. With the help of right type of questions a wise teacher can lead the students from dark and unknown regions to known and bright ones.

Good Vitality. In the opinion of Arthur B. Moehlman, "Good vitality is essential to successful teaching, not only in its reflex influence upon the children but also in making possible continuity of work with the fewest possible interruptions from illness because of general fatigue."

Use of Material Aids. Various teaching aids bring clarity and vividness. It is a great asset to the teacher to narrate stories and anecdotes which appeal to children at different ages and attainment levels. Abstract words and phrases can be made clear by illustrations.

Good Memory. A teacher with a poor memory is ridiculous. It becomes easier for a teacher having good memory to correlate many things. A good creative memory is one of the qualities that differentiates the good teacher from the mediocre.

Good Voice. The voice of a teacher should be clear, moderately pitched and well-modulated. A thin low voice develops dullness and monotony in the class. A very high pitched voice or shrill one must be avoided. It distracts the minds of the students and does not appeal to their aesthetic sense. Plenty of variety must be introduced in voice. A teacher must be slow and emphatic when he is making statements he thinks worth copying. No effort should be spared to cultivate a pleasant musical tone. Anything which adds pleasure is an additional attraction for the attention and especially with children.

The intelligent teacher should know the value of pause. He should know when to raise his voice and when to drop it a little or when to drop it altogether. He should adjust his voice according to the size of the room. Often a good speech fails because it cannot be easily heard especially by those who sit at the back. But it does not mean that a teacher should always be shouting. There are three ways of changing the voice—in pitch, in loudness and in speed.

Optimistic Outlook. Dr. E.A. Pires thinks that the teacher who can infuse happiness into the work of his students because he himself enjoys his work is sure to be a successful and popular teacher.

According to S. Balakrishna Joshi, "A teacher whose soul is wrinkled and whose heart is atrophied, who is devoid of energy and enthusiasm, capacity and character and who simply marks time, his eyes fixed on the calendar, is a disgrace to the profession and a curse on society." "The great teacher lives and breathes the spirit of creativity and adventure," writes Dr. E.A. Pires.

Laughter. A tactful teacher never hesitates to laugh, when there is an occasion for it. Laughter done in an unhealthy spirit defeats its own purpose. A teacher should never make the mistake of laughing at the students. He should laugh with them and should also see that they laugh with him and not at him.

R.R. Kumaria thinks laughter to be embellishment that lends charm to the teaching profession.

Humour keeps the students attentive. A very wise teacher once remarked, "I consider a day's teaching is wasted if we do not at all have a hearty laugh." Sarcasm is to be avoided.

Thirst for Knowledge. A teacher must refresh himself by constant reading not only about his subjects but books which touch life at every point. It would be very helpful if he would get opportunities of attending educational seminars, refresher courses and the. like which enable him to get a good grip of his own thoughts and to see his own working in relation to others in the same sphere.

"A teacher can never truly teach unless he is still learning himself" remarks Rabindra Nath Tagore. A teacher should not feel shy to learn from others. There is no end to knowledge and his attitude should be like that of Newton: "I am only a child, playing in the sand by the sea-shore, picking up a pebble here and there with a vast ocean of truth lying undiscovered before me."

Books, Magazines and Newspapers. Although he should read books, magazines and newspapers for his own enjoyment and profit he must keep in mind his responsibilities as a teacher. His reading must be wide enough so that he can guide his students' reading tastes.

Travel. The summer vacation usually is regarded rightly by most teachers as a period of deserved and needed rest and relaxation. However, an interested and efficient teacher is primarily a teacher for twelve months of the year. Even during his period of relaxation he makes it a point to combine pleasure with education. During summer, winter or spring vacations teachers can visit historical or literary landmarks in their immediate environment. Returning to their classes they can share their experiences with their students, thus enriching the content of their subjects and stimulate their classes.

Membership of Professional Organizations. Teachers should become members of the professional organizations the functions of which are:

(a) To advance education ideals.

(b) To care for the welfare of children and young people.

(c) To safeguard the welfare of teachers.

(d) To improve teaching, supervisory, and administrative procedures.

(e) To improve salaries.

(f) To assure pension and tenure privileges.

(g) To secure for teachers the right to participate in educational policy-making.

In Service Training. Refresher courses, seminars and workshops provide opportunities for the discussion of classroom problems and find out their solutions. They also come into contact with their co-workers who might have something new to say. This also enables them to keep in touch with the latest developments in the field of education.

Punctuality. A teacher must realize that coming late to school and going late to the class upsets the school work, causes indiscipline and undermines the tone of the school. A good teacher makes it a point to be punctual in every work. Following the teachers coming late, the student may also develop in himself this very habit.

Judicious Use of the Praise and Blame. Praise and blame are the two important weapons in the armoury of the teacher and these should be used very judiciously. "Praise like gold and diamond owes its value to scarcity writes Robinson Johnson.

A word of praise or commendation will easily enhance the students' interest in any course of action. Praise, rightly employed, is a forceful incentive at the disposal of the teacher.

Rebukes and scoldings are also to be used very sparingly, otherwise they lose their value.

Patience. He has to deal with a large number of students having low and high power of understanding. He may have to repeat his lessons many a time for the sake of the less intelligent and he should not be irritated in doing so. Some students, by nature, pick up lessons very slowly and a teacher should possess the required patience to make them understand gradually. Good habits are not formed overnight. It requires time and patience to inculcate virtues in the students.

Justice and Impartiality. The teacher should not show undue favour to some. All should be equal in his eyes. Undue favour to some students will lead to frustration among others.

True to his Commands. Less commands should be given to the students and when given, they must be stuck to otherwise they lose their effectiveness.

Free from Political Bias. The students should not be exploited for political purposes. The programmes of the various political parties must be placed before them in their true perspective.

Free from Religious Fanaticism. The minds of the young should not be poisoned through narrow-mindedness and bigotry. The partition of the country has shown what wrong fanaticism can do.

Sense of Patriotism. If a teacher does not possess a sense of patriotism, he would not be successful in his attempts to develop love for the country in the students.

Always Alive to the Aims of Education. Never for a moment should the teacher forget that the aim of education is not to prepare child for Matriculation or any other examination but to inculcate in him the quality of head, heart, hand and health.

Regarding this Dr. E.A. Pires writes, "He has to concern himself with the total development of the child and not only with one or two aspects, must be friend to him and help him in his emotional and social developments, he must be a philosopher illumining the way of his intellectual and spiritual progress, he must be his guide in his moral and aesthetic advancement. In fact, he must be 'all things' to all his students, a physician concerned about their physical health, a mental hygienist leading them carefully to sound mental health, a philosopher guiding them painstakingly in their search for truth, a moralist assisting and encouraging them to acquire goodness, an artist helping them to find beauty. In fact he must be minister ministering to their every need, such a ministry calls for dedicated service."

Interest in Co-curricular Activities. It is needless to stress the importance of co-curricular activities in the present system of education. They are perhaps more important than the traditional subject. And as such a teacher can hardly afford to be indifferent to this aspect of school life.

Missionary. Dr. E. A. Pires opines that the great teacher has the zeal of a missionary. There is a certain aptness in the analogy between a missionary and a teacher, for every true missionary is first and last a teacher.

S. Balakrishna Joshi feels, "Without a band of devoted teachers who are inspired by a holy-zeal, an institution with the paraphernalia of modern convenience will be like a beautiful corpse without spark of life, a carcass without soul." According to the same author teaching is a divinely ordained mission.

Teacher as a Guide. Child being the 'Hero in the drama of education' must be allowed to play an active role in the process of education. "The teacher is a guide and director, he steers the boat but the energy that propels it must come from those who are learning," remarks Dewey. Similarly, Shri Aurobindo writes, "The first principle of true teaching is that nothing can be taught. The teacher is not an instructor or a task master, he is a helper and a guide. His business is to suggest and not to impose. He does not actually train the student's mind, he shows him how to perfect his instruments of knowledge and helps and encourages him in the process. He does not impart knowledge to him; he shows him how to acquire knowledge for himself. He does not call forth the knowledge that is within; he only shows him where it lies and how it can be habituated to rise to the surface."

Prayer of Unknown Teacher. Henry Van Dyke writes, "I sing the praise of the unknown teacher. Great generals win campaigns but it is the unknown soldier who wins the war. Famous educators plan new systems of pedagogy, but it is the unknown teacher who directs and guides the young. He lives in obscurity and contends with hardship. For him no trumpets blare, no chariots wait, no golden decorations are decreed. He keeps the watch along the borders of darkness and makes the attack on the trenches of ignorance and folly. Patient in his daily life, he strives to conquer the evil powers which are the enemies of youth. He awakens sleeping spirits. He quickens the indolent, encourages the eager, and steadies the unstable. He communicates his own joy in learning and shares with boys and girls the best treasures of his mind. He lights many candies, which in later years will shine back to cheer him. This is his reward. Knowledge may be gained from books, but the law of knowledge is transmitted only by personal contact. No one has ever deserved better of republic than the unknown teacher. No one is more worthy to be enrolled in a democratic aristocracy, "King of himself and servant of mankind."

MUTUAL RELATIONSHIPS

Relation with Students

1. Respects the individuality of the
2. Recognizes individual differences.
3. Works for the welfare of all.
4. Refrains from tutoring for remuneration.
5. Shows impartial treatment with all.
6. Refrains from imposing his religions or political convictions upon his students.

Relation with Associates

1. Believes in mutual help and cooperation.
2. Gives due credit for assistance received and achievement accomplished.
3. Refrains from interfering in the affairs of his colleagues unless official duties warrant.
4. Refrains from shifting, responsibility to others which should be borne by himself.
5. Refrains from criticising his fellow teachers.
6. Helps his colleagues with helpful ideas and constructive advice.
7. Organizes properly and leaving for his successor such information, data and records as may be required in beginning the next year's work.

Relation with the Profession

1. Shows a personal pride in the teaching profession.
2. Helps in raising standards of entrance to the profession.
3. Shows an open mind towards all forms of professional conduct.
4. Broadens his educational equipment for teaching after entering the profession.
5. Becomes an active member of the professional organizations.
6. Refrains from getting unearned favours from publishers.
7. Works for material conditions necessary for a high degree of professional service.

8. Honours any contract entered into.
9. Extends full cooperation to authorities.

TIPS FOR TEACHERS

Teaching Procedures and Methods

1. Prepare your lesson thoroughly.
2. Plan your work systematically.
3. Have everything ready to start classwork and be sure you get the attention of every member of the class.
4. Make assignments definite and clear.
5. Use a variety of teaching aids.
6. Word questions clearly so that the students know what you are asking from them.
7. Teach the whole class and not a few students sitting on the front benches.
8. Do not often repeat your questions.
9. Do not put questions hurriedly.
10. Distribute questions evenly.
11. Put questions to inattentive students also.
12. Allow reasonable time to the students to answer your questions.
13. Encourage students to answer questions rather than having you do all the talking.
14. Provide opportunities for all students to participate.
15. Avoid being side tracked.
16. Check the written work of the students carefully.

17. Encourage students to report on anything of current interest to them and the class, which pertains to the course.
18. Make necessary explanations about corrected assignments.
19. Vary methods of teaching and learning; use dramas, panel discussion, debate, etc.
20. Make your black-board writing legible.
21. Avoid difficult assignments when you first begin.
22. Allow supervised study time.
23. Keep the students always busy in doing some worthwhile work.
24. Make every student feel that he is essential to the success of the lesson.
25. Make every effort to avoid all suggestions of criticism or anger before group.
26. Make a judicious use of praise, and blame to the class as a whole and to individual members.
27. Explain errors to student individually rather than before a whole class, when an individual is concerned.
28. Provide problem situations by putting thought provoking questions.

Classroom Routine

1. Tell your name carefully and accurately.
2. Learn the names of the students quickly.
3. Learn carefully the seating plan of students.
4. Keep room well-ventilated and lighted.

5. Take the roll-call and enquire about the absentees.
6. Keep an accurate record of absentees and tardiness.
7. Maintain a neat room.
8. Acquaint yourself with procedures and forms of school.
9. Insist on correct postures.
10. Impress upon the students the importance of respect for school property.
11. Be always punctual.
12. Stand throughout the great part of the class period.
13. Have a definite system for collecting and distributing materials to avoid confusion.
14. Rub off the black-board when you leave the classroom.
15. Train your students to keep themselves busy when you are not in the classroom.
16. Collect materials and books as soon as the period is over.
17. Do not leave anything in disorder when you leave the class.

Guidance and Counselling

1. Be acquainted with the home conditions of the child.
2. Recognise individual differences.
3. Develop feeling of friendliness so that every student feels free to ask your assistance in personal and school problems.
4. Be available for student conferences.

5. Study health records, test scores, anecdotal records, etc., of each student.
6. Share your knowledge and understanding of students with other teachers.
7. Maintain up-to-date cumulative records.
8. Evince continued interest in assisting students to solve their problems.
9. Take interest in testing programmes.
10. Cooperate with other guidance workers for finding satisfactory solutions.

Class Discipline

1. Base your discipline on do's rather than don'ts.
2. Use the standards of the group as a foundation of your disciplinary measures.
3. Be sympathetic and understanding in your dealings with students.
4. Be firm and consistent in your dealing with students.
5. Do not allow students to wander around.
6. Insist on good conduct or manners and high standards of work.
7. Maintain a certain reserve and be friendly rather than achummy'.
8. Be just and fair.
9. Avoid telling the class to keep order.
10. Avoid abusive language.
11. Avoid sarcastic remarks.
12. Avoid threats.

13. Attend to minor problems before they become major ones.
14. Try to adopt and extend this philosophy, "I like you even though, I do not like what you do."
15. Encourage respect and honesty.
16. Make every effort to solve your own disciplinary problems.
17. Refer cases of indiscipline to the higher authorities when you must.
18. Do not discuss your family problems in the classroom.
19. Do not discuss your colleagues with the students.
20. Do not narrate your experiences too often.

Personality Traits

1. Be punctual in your programmes.
2. Do not use loud voice.
3. Be always cheerful.
4. Handle controversial topics skilfully.
5. Avoid mannerism.
6. Be humorous.
7. Use polite and proper language.
8. Be well-mannered.
8. Avoid sarcastic remarks.
10. Show sincere interest in students, school activities and coworkers.
11. Be frank to admit "Don't know all the answers."
12. Cultivate initiative and resourcefulness.
13. Be true to the ethics of the teaching profession.

To play his role effectively and efficiently, a teacher is expected to understand the significance of the following and act accordingly:

Who is to Teach. The teacher is to teach and he must know his strengths and weaknesses and should strive to present reasonably good models before his students.

Whom to Teach? The teacher should understand his students thoroughly, their aptitudes, abilities, habits, manners and temperaments and accordingly cater to their needs.

Why to Teach? He should always remember that the aim of education is to develop harmonious personalities, who are culturally refined, emotionally stable, ethically sound, mentally alert, morally upright, physically strong, socially efficient and spiritually enlightened. He should not forget even for a moment that the traditional 3 R's have been replaced by 7 R's, *i.e.* Reading, Writing, Arithmetic, Recreation, Rights, Responsibilities and Relationships.

Where to Teach? He ought not to think that school is not merely a place of imparting information but a place where men of tomorrow are trained to take up their proper place in the society and contribute to national development.

What to Teach? He must know his subject well.

How to Teach? He must make use of new technology in the teaching learning process.

When to Teach? He should develop motivation among his students to make his teaching effective and inspirational.

❋❋❋

9

Planning Process

Realizing the need for institutional planning the Education Commission 1964-66 observed:

> "No comprehensive programme of educational development can ever be put across unless it involves every educational institution and tall the human factors connected with it-its teachers, students and the local community and unless it provides the necessary inducement, to make them put in their best efforts."

What is an Institutional Plan? Mr. M.B. Buch describes it as a programme of development and improvement prepared by an educational institution on the basis of its felt needs and the resources available or likely to be available with a view to improve the school programme and school practices. The plan may be for a longer duration or a shorter duration. It is based on the principle of optimum utilisation of the resources available in the school and community.

Significant Features

1. The plan is prepared of the needs of the school as identified by the school staff.
2. It is a cooperative venture of the community, management, school staff and the students.
3. It is goal-oriented.

4. It is based on the principle of optimum utilization of resources available within the school and the community.

5. It results into establishment of democratic procedures within the school.

6. It is specific for an institution. There cannot be a single plan for all the institutions.

7. An important outcome of institutional planning is the establishment of a better rapport with the community.

8. It forms the basis of the District Plan for educational development and improvement.

9. It aims at school improvement as well as school development.

10. It results into improvement—motivation on the part of teachers, students, community and the managements.

Main Stress on Motivating the Human Agencies. The Education Commission felt:

"In our opinion therefore the emphasis in this movement should be not so much on physical resources as on motivating the human agencies concerned to make their best efforts in a coordinated manner for the improvement of education and there by offset the shortcomings in the physical resources."

Programmes Based on Human Effort and not Physical Effort. The Commission suggested the following programmes:

1. Reduction in stagnation and wastage.

2. Improvement of teaching methods.

3. Assistance to retarded students.

4. Trying out new techniques of work.
5. Special assistance to gifted students.
6. Improved methods of organizing programme of the school.
7. Increasing the professional competence of teachers through programmes of self-study.

Positive Aspects

Institutional planning is required to make the educational planning into the country more realistic. It reverses the normal trend followed today where the direction of the planning is from top to bottom. Institutional planning will give the right direction to the educational planning in the country, *i.e.*, the upward direction from bottom to top.

Institutional planning is a recognition of the role of practitioners of education in the process of planning education in the country.

Institutional planning introduces a scientific approach to the improvement and development of education within a country.

The Importance

Mr. J.T. Naik explains the significance of institutional planning as: "It is hardly worthwhile to discuss whether this idea is old or new. The more important question is whether it is relevant to our present situation. My humble submission is that it is. In this process of magnifying the scope of educational planning we have unfortunately lost sight of the individual institution and of its uniqueness, which necessitates planning at that level. It is to correct this mistake that we propose to develop this programme of institutional planning in which we want to pay adequate attention to the macrocosm, the individual institution, without forgetting the wider horizon, the macrocosm of State and national planning."

Spirit of Institutional Planning. Dr. Shib K. Mitra outlines the spirit of institutional plan as: "I think the whole notion of institutional planning is based on this idea that at every stage right from the school to this topmost level in the field of education constant effort has to be made in order that we do not have new ideas for the sake of new ideas but in order that we can do a better job with whatever resources we have at our command."

Institutional Planning as a Basic Link in the Planning Process. Dr. B.D. Nag Chaudhari explains it as, "I would like to reiterate that planning for each institution provides an important and basic link in the planning process. To derive the benefits of such detailed planning at the micro-operational level, it has to be linked appropriately with the planning at the District, State and Central levels. We can then formulate an integrated National Educational Policy which will be responsive to the changes of the situation and incorporate within it the seeds of gradual improvement. While the planning at the State and national levels deals with the formulation of national goals, priorities and weaning out disparities, the implementation of programmes, the evolution of new programmes, experimentation on new techniques, discovery of talents and guidance are major task at the institutional level. Since the implementation of the plans and programmes is as important and vital as plan formulation, institutional planning has a special contribution to make in national development. Planning for each school and college has an advantage that it brings to the plan formulation process a realism, an appreciation of the felt needs of the community and an awareness of the difficulties and problems at the operational level."

How to Prepare a School Plan? The major steps in preparing a plan of improvement and development for a school are:

(i) Undertaking a survey of the needs of the school.

(ii) Undertaking a survey of the resources available in the school as well as community.

(iii) Preparing plans of improvement programmes, and

(iv) Evaluating improvement programmes.

Institutional Improvement Plans at the District Level. The District Educational Officer will receive the institutional plans from the different schools within his jurisdiction. This will give him a detailed picture of the improvement projects undertaken by the schools in the district. This will also give him an idea of the in service training needs of the teachers in his district. A useful analysis and consolidation of the various institutional plans at the district level will tell the D.E.O. the following:

1. Type of improvement projects going on in the school.
2. The way he will try to bring about coordination between similar projects going on in different schools.
3. The overall in-service education needs of the teachers in his district and how he will obtain the services of the nearby Extension Services Department for organizing the courses in different subjects for the teachers of his district.
4. The financial requirements over the period of next 5 years if the minimum essential developments are to be financed.

The D.E.O. will keep institutional plans with him while going out for usual inspection. He will be in a position to study the progress of various improvement projects and also he will be in a position to disseminate the successful programmes of different schools to all the schools in the District.

A seminar on Institutional Planning was organized jointly by the National Council of Educational Research and Training and the Ministry of Education, Government of India in seminar at the Regional College of Education, Bhopal, provided an opportunity to the participants, among whom were Inspecting Offices, staff members of Training Colleges and heads of Secondary Schools deputed by some State Governments to discuss the concept and methodology of institutional planning with several experts in the field.

School Principals and Institutional Planning. Improvement means change. It is necessary for a principal to know that the school does not consist of furniture and equipment only. The Principal should realize that the school has a social system and to bring about a change in a social system has its own complexities. As a social system the school has various aspects like goals, established procedures, different subject groups, relationship among the various subject groups and its own norms. An attempt to change one aspect of the school life will influence and disturb the overall school equilibrium.

The first job of the Principal should be to look at the whole school system, assess the strengths and weaknesses of his staff member's and carefully create the ground work for various changes. He will have to proceed in a planned manner.

Various Steps

Individual and Group Conferences. The first step might be a series of individual conferences with the staff followed by group conference. After this there might be a staff meeting in which the Principal and outside experts may explain the whole purpose and the needs for preparing an institutional plan. The Principal shall take a close look as to how the suggestions in the staff meetings are received by the teachers. In other words, he will evaluate the result of the first staff meeting.

Discussions with Teachers and Experts. The second step will be a discussion about undertaking a survey of the needs of improvement and development of the school. This will be a longer process as most teachers find it difficult to identify the real problems. Experts from outside, senior teachers and the Principal himself will have to work with individual teachers and subject teachers groups to have the survey of the real needs felt by the school staff for improvement in various areas. It will be necessary for the Principal to list the areas requiring improvement in a proper sequence from the view point of available resources and the nature of difficulties involved in implementing the programmes. The Principal will always encourage teachers to take up such programmes as can be completed by the teachers without much difficulty. It is the success in the initial programmes that will inspire confidence for undertaking major improvement programmes.

Survey of Resources. The third step will be a survey of the resources available in the school and the community. Here again greater stress will be laid on knowing, what already exists in the school.

Preparation of Improvement Programmes. The fourth step will be preparation of improvement programmes. Here adequate reading material, reference materials, expert guidance shall have to be provided to teachers planning improvement programmes. Each improvement programme will take the form of a project and guidelines of preparing projects will be supplied to the teachers by the Principal.

Evaluation of the Programme. The fifth step will be the evaluation of the programmes after they have been implemented and completed. In fact the Principal will carryon periodical evaluation of the various programmes and staff consultative surveys of the teachers to modify the procedures if need is felt for it.

The Scope

Academic Programmes. Here, improvement of instructional programmes and enrichment of curriculum should be included to improve the school results both in the home examinations as well as in external examination by reducing wastage and stagnation, improving the attendance ratio, improving ways of home assignment etc.

Co-curricular Area. Here a programme of school beautification, creating an environment which can stimulate learning by students, physical education programmes, co-curricular programmes etc. should be included.

School Services. There is an urgent need to prepare a planned programme for the improvement and utilization of library service, laboratory service and guidance services, etc. Other services which directly concern the students welfare like the mid-day meal, drinking water, sanitation and hygiene should also be planned for improvement.

In-service Programmes and Professional Growth of Teachers. This is an important area for planning. A plan for the professional growth of individual teacher should be prepared. Programmes for the in-service education of teachers and group programmes for the in-service education of the entire school faculty should be prepared in a planned way. Stress should be laid on the in-service needs of the individual teachers.

Maximum Utilization of School Resources. This is an area which is the most important for any programme of institutional planning. There are schools which have surplus teachers without adequate work. There are schools which have teachers not fitting into the curriculum offerings. There are schools which have shortage of teachers. The institutional planning should aim at maximum utilization of all available teacher resources. The planning should also aim at utilizing the unutilized teaching aids, the building facilities, the playgrounds, etc. A good institutional plan should study this area of human and physical resources and their maximum utilisation for the improvement of the school.

EDUCATIONAL LEADERSHIP

Planning Stage

1. The first step for the District Educational Officer is to create an awareness amongst the Heads of Institutions for institutional planning and its importance by calling a meeting of the heads of schools at the district level.

2. The heads of institutions will be asked to prepare improvement and development plans on the basis of felt needs and availability of resources in consultation with the teachers, students and the local community and fix priorities. Every school will, however, be required to put up a minimum action plan.

3. The autonomy of the schools in institutional planning, implementation and to a certain extent in evaluation is a must at all stages, it being their own plan.

4. The plan will be phased according to the extent, need and resources, which should be normally for one academic session, which may be the duration of the plan.

5. The District Educational Officer will have the advisory role to play with regard to the institutional plans and he will be helped by an academic cell which may be created in his office. This cell will consist of subject experts, specialists in guiding research workers, who will be associated with the plan at all stages. The cell will provide expert advice from time to time according to the needs of the school.

6. The District Educational Officer will extend help and guidance to the schools promptly when the schools ask for it.
7. The District Educational Officer will ensure recognition of good work at different levels. The Directorate will also encourage good workers.

Practical Aspects

1. D.E.O. will arrange publicity of the state and national plans as far as they relate to and affect the schools and the teachers.
2. He will use his influence and good offices in tapping local resources, different agencies and enlisting community help for the implementation of the plans.
3. He will encourage inter-school visits for exchange of ideas and provide T.A. and D.A. facilities.
4. He being a very important link between the schools and the department, will secure financial aid for the schools wherever needed to encourage good work and if the requirements of the plan so demand.
5. He will provide resource personnel from the district, extension services and from outside.
6. He would arrange for in-service training of teachers in areas of institutional planning.
7. He will help in getting the students' fund rules liberalized to facilitate utilization of funds by the head of the institution with the help of the school committee setup for the purpose.
8. Due publicity will be arranged for good plans and significant individual work, through school and district bulletins, departmental journals, conferences and seminars.

Self-evaluation. The school community will make appraisal of the entire plan programme chalked out, targets achieved, difficulties experienced. This will be done frequently and modifications made to make it more practicable and useful.

Supervision and Inspection. The D.E.A. and the panel inspection team comprising of experienced headmasters (including retired personnel) will evaluate the programme at least once a year or more if possible.

The evaluation will be done by the learn in terms of the extent of contribution of creative ideas in planning, resourcefulness shown in implementation—the depth of their qualities as well as the number of people involved in making their contribution. This should be helpful in judging as to how far the plan has been successful. A scrutiny will be made by examining the process and the produce.

The success of institutional planning, implementation· and proper evaluation will depend on the dynamic leadership, initiative and personality of the D.E.A. He will be instrumental in encouraging good work by securing special development grants for the schools on the basis of the performance.

10

Training for Teachers

The progress of a country depends upon the quality of its teachers and for this reason teaching is the noblest among all professions. The irony of fate, however, is that teaching is the most unattractive profession and teacher no longer occupies an honourable position in the society. Teaching can regain its earlier noble status in case the quality of teacher-education in our country is improved. It is probably for this reason that the Education Commission recommends the introduction of "a sound programme of professional education of teachers".

The Commission further remarks that investment in teacher education can yield very rich dividends because the resources required are small when measured against the resulting improvements in the education of millions. In the absence of other influences, a teacher tries to teach in the way in which he himself was taught by his favourite teacher and this tends to perpetuate the traditional methods of teaching in a situation like the present when new and dynamic methods of instruction are needed such an attitude becomes an obstacle in progress. He can be modified only by effective professional education

Basis Issues

Both terms have different meanings. The term 'training' has very limited boundary while education is a very broad term under which many things come.

Training. This term is specially defined and explained in the glossary of training terms published in 1971 in London by the department of employment. In this glossary training has been defined as "Systematic, development of attitude, knowledge, skill, behaviour patterns required by an individual in order to perform adequately a given job or task."

Knowledge. 'Bruner' in "Instructional Technology" has defined the term as "Knowledge consists of facts, concepts, terms, principles, theories, generalization, etc., which are useful for a teacher."

A teacher must have knowledge of his subject, methods and techniques of teaching and factors which affect teaching and knowledge of child psychology.

For training purpose it is necessary to know which part of knowledge is essential depending upon the nature of the job.

Attitude. Attitudes are emotionalized mental state towards his job. It involves feeling about something and this feeling aspect is very important. The favourable attitude is very necessary in order to succeed the job. Favourable attitudes make better performance. A teacher with favourable attitude can force his students to learn more. Teacher must have positive, healthy and favourable attitude towards his job, his students, society and other related components of job; only then he can succeed in his job otherwise not.

Skills. Skills are specific behaviour or activities which an individual requires to do a particular job or task. It refers to the doing part of the human. The manner in which he has to do the work is the skill of questioning, skill of illustrating demonstrating, etc.

Behaviour Patterns. Behaviour patterns are style of functioning or working and style of functioning differs from job to job. Training emphasizes specific attitude specific knowledge, and specific Skills. Efficient performance of the job depends upon the training. Objective of training programme is also very specific.

Education. All kinds of activities which aim at developing the knowledge, moral values and understandings required in the work of life constitute what we mean to be education.

The purpose of education is to develop well informed, well intensive and well equipped-citizen of the society. And the purpose of education is to develop the human being not an individual alone. There are qualities of general nature as the sense, that are needed by everyone in respect of the job he is engaged in. There are qualities required by everyone to live a good life, well adjusted and harmonious life. These all qualities are developed by education.

Education is a wider term that goes beyond the boundaries of one particular job. It also emphasizes knowledge, skill and attitude but these are of a general nature which may be useful in more than one job and also important from the point of view of the large community or society. Education emphasizes general, important and refinement in behaviour, development of a personality, development of a person who has interest in wider aspect of his environment. Education emphasizes development of knowledge, understanding values and behaviours which are required in all walks of life.

The Pattern

'Glaser', in his book 'Psychological Instructional Technology in Training, Research and Education' published by University of Pitsburg has pointed out that a distinction can be made in training and education on the basis of two criteria:

(a) The degree of specificity of objectives.

(b) Minimizing *vs.* Maximizing individual differences.

Training has more specific objectives and attempts to minimize individual difference while educational objectives are more general and it maximizes the individual differences. It means when people are educated the difference among them are increased and when they are trained differences are minimized.

DIFFERENCE BETWEEN EDUCATION AND TRAINING

Education	*Training*
1. Education emphasized the activities which aim at developing the knowledge and moral values required in all walks of life rather than knowledge and skill relating to only a limited field of activities. Education is a process of developing integrated personality.	1. It emphasizes on development of specific knowledge, attitude, skills and behaviour patterns which an individual requires to perform a job adequately. These behaviour patterns differ from job to job. If we train a teacher we develop those skills which are needed for him to be a good teacher.
2. The purpose of education is to provide the conditions essential for young persons and adults to develop an understanding of traditions and ideas influencing the society in which they live, others cultures and of the law of nature and to acquire linguistic and other skills which are basic to learning personal development and creativity.	2. The purpose of Training is to bring excellence. in the specific job for which the individuals being trained. Training is concerned with people learning to perform tasks fairly specific and prescribed tasks, although there are exceptions where tasks are more opened as in management and supervision.

Difference in education and training exits more in the context of instructional activity than the actual methods used and objectives sought. Nevertheless academically it is impossible to make clear distinction between training and education. Training is an aspect of education.

The Importance

Training is necessary for efficient work in a particular job.

If we appoint a person in any job after sometime through apprentice he will be quite competent for that job. If a person is trained before employing him in a job this is called pre-training. This pre-training is very important. Without providing any training if we employ a person in a job then it is risky because he does not have any knowledge about the machine, when a person fails in a job he develops negative attitude towards the job and thinks that he is not competent for that job.

Therefore the pre-training is must. By having some training he will get success in his job with full satisfaction.

There is need for training in general:

1. In order to perform the job successfully and effectively.
2. It is seen that a trained person learns effectively in a lesser time than untrained person. A person can learn these things without training also when he is in job but efforts and time will go waste and he may learn many irrelevant things also.
3. Organized and systematic programme of training makes them to learn easily in a more efficient way in lesser time.
4. More complex jobs require more specific knowledge, attitude, and skills and behaviour patterns that more specificity is there hence training is more important in these jobs. The risk is involved if he learns on job even it may cause danger to his life also and secondly trial and error results into wastage of time and energy. A good deal of waste of efforts can be saved through training.

Teacher Education

Certain people, who are not in favour of training hold the view that there is no need of training the teachers, only they should have mastery over the subject because there is no significant difference found in teaching of training and untrained person.

Theoretically it is not right. Training is essential for every teacher. Trained teachers can do much more than untrained teachers. There may be so many reasons for that why they do not perform their work effectively. Demand of job/profession, the objective and expectations from a teacher certify the existence of teachers' training.

To have mastery over subject matter and to communicate this to students are quite different. Many skills are needed to communicate the information effectively *e.g.*, skill of questioning illustrating, demonstrating and explaining, etc., other skills which may be required are skill of arranging and logically sequencing the subject-matter.

Teaching is not confined to tell or to impart knowledge of subject matter to others but in wider perspective teaching aims at all round development of personality of child. But there are the things to be taught to the teacher, *e.g.*, what his responsibilities and duties etc. are. These things or skills or attitudes can only be developed through systematic training. Hence a systematized knowledge is required in order to achieve these skills and attitudes. For this training is must.

There is not only the knowledge of these things which are, essential for a teacher unless a person has a positive attitude towards students and his job. Attitudes are learnt through experiences. In training programme many pleasant experiences are provided to student teacher by which he can develop favourable attitude towards himself, his job and his students.

The skills require more practice. Many specific skills have been identified which are to be developed in teacher trainees and these can only be developed by systematic programme of teachers' training.

So theoretical need for training the teacher has some rationale. The technical knowledge and skill can be developed in the teacher through training. Therefore, training is necessary for all type of teachers.

Higher Level Training. Need for training for primary and secondary teachers has been emphasized by many commissions and committees but there are few who realize the need for training the college-teachers also.

In the past, it had been advocated that need for high-school and junior high-school teachers' training and for degree colleges there is no need of training. But now-a-days, a feeling is growing up in the circle of top educationists that there should be need for training for college-teachers also. The idea has been propagated by top educators particularly by N.C.T.E. But prior to this U.G.C. has also organized certain type of orientation programmes for college teachers. In the beginning there was a great resistance of this idea. Now more and more people working in universities and professional colleges are accepting this idea and advocating the need for training.

Actually, the whole universe of teachers in the country is divided into two groups:

1. Training does not make a person more effective.
2. Who have great faith in training, say if training has not produced effective teachers perhaps it might be due to several other reasons. If training is organized it must produce effective teachers. They organized seminars on different universities on teacher-education.

In 1971, U.G.C. funded a larger number of programmes of orientation teaching. U.G.C. asked various universities to hold summer course for orienting college and university-teachers.

During five year plans a huge fund is allocated for the professional improvement of college teachers by seminar, refresher courses, orientation courses, evening courses, summer courses, etc.

Relationship between training and job is helping the people to be more successful on job. If we put people on job having that knowledge and skills which are required for job, predication will be successful.

Teaching is a profession which needs training. But at what level teaching needs training, this is the questions. Teaching at any level is done with a view to impart knowledge. So far as objectives are concerned they do not vary at various levels. Only content and procedure is changed at different levels.

Besides mastery of subject many other things are developed through training. Training astonishes several things for effective teaching.

In the past few years this need has been greatly emphasized and voiced and gradually we have reached to a conclusion that some sort of training is essential for college-teachers also. All above evidences are sufficient to conclude that there must be some sort of training for college-teachers also.

Educating Teachers

All the teachers should be trained, but there should not be and also cannot be a specific training of teachers. This conviction is born out by observations that even the born teachers have to study the techniques of teaching craft. There are teachers who through training and experiences have acquired enormous success in teaching. There is, however, no denying the fact that much wastage in teaching-effort can be saved if the prospective teacher is subjected to teacher-education for actualisation of potential in him.

A good deal of waste in teaching-efforts might be avoided by training. It is a further reason that a teacher might be trained. But a teacher is not a teaching craftsman. He has to help his students to develop certain personality traits and also to realize desirable values. This means that there should not be specific training of teachers. An era of the training teachers is past. It was born out of the necessity to bring up a literate generation and to accomplish this task. The teachers were helped to develop a narrow technique and a, highly specialized professional approach. Today, the need is to bring out a 'sophisticated' and 'cultured' generation, and to accomplish this task a new type of men and women are demanded. The very phrase "the trainee teacher" is out of date. Training is commonly associated with *ad hoc* preparation for an absolute content or with teaching tricks for animal or with a narrow vocationalism.

The schools of today generally lay emphasis on an integrated and balanced personality of the teacher as a whole man. The teacher of today, must be the teacher of a whole man, and he can never be this unless he himself is a complete man. We teach more by our actions than by our preaching.

Training cannot be a matter of teaching professional tricks, and the student who comes to the training institution should try his best to learn these tricks. A narrow vocationalism is wholly out of tune with modern educational thought, and it is antipathetic to those generous sympathies and that consciousness of being one member in a self-education community which is generally demanded from teachers.

Many teachers' training institutions are producing humanly illiterate teachers who are not able to cope up with the aspirations of rising generation of youth who will be required to meet the human encounters. The new teacher will have to integrate the skills of teaching with his life style and also to help the students to develop not only intellectually but also emotionally.

The tragedy is that teacher in general adopt little real character or work of whom we entrust to bring up children in an ideal way.

Teachers are a section of community sharply segregated from the rest of the community preparing themselves for their life's work in institutions where their fellow students will be preparing themselves for developing human attributes They have little opportunity and less encouragement to share m the enjoyment of things by which a man lives. The tea education system as it exists today may succeed in the training of teachers but it has entirely failed to educate the h beings. This is what we have tended to do. The train has been too often the untrained human being. This process, therefore, must be reversed. Our aim must be the education of the right human beings for work in our schools. If we can succeed in this, the trained teachers will follow. An era of the training of teachers is past; our concern 'today' is with the education of the educators.

Then, who is the human being that we need? His chief characteristic, if there is any thing in him, must be wholeness of personality, mind and wholeness of experience. With proper type of education to the prospective teacher, he will be in a more favourable position to correlate his knowledge with experience, to see life steadily and to see it as a whole. His mature study of child's growth process will strengthen his intellect. The only means of strengthening one's intellect Keats has said is to let the mind be a thoroughfare for all thoughts, not a selected party. From this open-mindedness, sympathy, tolerance, intellectual adaptability and that width of interest will spring the attributes which are essential for successful living and to deal with children. But all this requires, a comprehensive goal to deal with. This implies a philosophy of life and education, a map by which the future teacher may see himself in relation to other teachers as well as other human beings activities.

It means that he must be given time and opportunity during his training course to think about education because he will have little time to think about education after completing his training. After the completion of his teacher-education course, he will be engaged in the all absorbing tasks of the classroom and the common life.

The prospective teacher, therefore, must be offered opportunities frequently to associate with the best minds and thereby to develop a disciplined intellect as well as the quality of appreciation of culture into all forms. This implies that he will have an emotional life developed to a fine sensitivity but held in a strict control.

The need of today's teacher is such a philosophy which is primarily concerned with human beings to interact with each other. In our humanistic programme for teacher-education we are attempting to develop a human teacher who possesses such qualities as spontaneity, acceptance, creativity and self-realization. This programme should give and opportunity to the prospective teacher in order to relate theory to practice to search for greater personal understanding of himself and for the learning process of children'.

It should help him to develop compassion for weakness in individuals and sensitivity for the needs of human beings. The most important product of such an approach will be a teacher who will be true for his feelings and he will be in a position to know how to help children to realize their potential. It is hoped this humanistic approach to teacher-education will produce teacher who will be able to halt the continued process of education of human potential in our schools.

Though methods can never be taught, but the methods adopted by other teachers can be studied. Such knowledge which is gained and combined with other considerations, the student will be able to tryout various approaches to his work and afterwards during the practical work of the course. This is so because a practising teacher generally evolves and polishes his own method. It should be indeed in practice and not in the lecture-room in order to acquire technical skills.

The teacher should possess such skills and competencies so that his task may be easy, useful and effective. He should know the techniques and procedures which should be adopted in his profession. He should think about the effective performance of his duties. The important task of education for the future is to improve the intellectual and technical competence in teachers.

Competence and professional skills are the very heart of the programme of teacher-education.

For this purpose, the following operations are needed to be taken:

1. Providing professional educated entrants to the profession in adequate numbers.
2. Maintaining or increasing the quality of entrants for the profession to satisfy society's needs. Whereas the first aim is quantitative, the second one is qualitative.

Professional education should focus on the person as an individual who is in practice and seek to broaden his human, that is his mental, moral and emotional capacities. The teacher should have a sound philosophy of education. He should have the knowledge of an adequate functioning of psychology. He should also have a dynamic sociological perspective.

The education which we want to provide to the teacher should be such which will be helpful in developing their inner capacity and power. Only such teachers will be capable in relating theoretical insight to practice and will be able to improve preparation programme. Besides this they will be effective practitioners in their profession.

The aim of teacher-education is to develop such competencies in the prospective teachers which will be useful for them in becoming a successful teacher.

It tends to increase the ability of the teacher to deal with a range of individual differences. Many teachers presently believe that their job is to develop certain basic skills in a group of youngsters at a given level of achievement. This type of teacher is no longer useful for the school.

The teacher of tomorrow should be one who can design a teaching situation which is conducive for the growth of students' mental health and develops in them a commitment to a set of values that is creativity and enquiry skill.

Now-a-days a teacher is in the urgent need of certain skills and competencies to develop and he is also in need of a new type of knowledge to development in knowledge and attitude, atmosphere and facility so that he may be in a position to make this task easy, fruitful and confirming for the demands of the students. His education, therefore, should be according to the necessities of the time and needs, of the society.

Some of competencies which need to be developed in the teacher are as below:

1. The ability to relate with the learning of one student, this includes diagnosis and individual instruction.
2. The ability to communicate with the individual as well as the group.

3. The ability to analyse group development interaction and to perform a leadership role in a group.
4. The ability to acquire knowledge and skill in a disciplined manner.
5. The ability to structure the acquired knowledge, this competency will enable the teacher to choose from his specialisation, the type of knowledge that is important for a particular individual or group. It should be commensurated with student's growth.

In the end, it can be said that teaching is based upon scholarship. Scholarship will be of little use unless the teacher will communicate his scholarship to his student. Today, the chief task of education should be to upgrade the intellectual and technical competence of the teacher. The teachers of today are in need of such an education which is new, constructive spontaneous and which is based upon new philosophy of life. This education should also emphasize on social urgency, social ideal and social livings.

Objectives and Goals

Education helps in the development of an individual's cognitive, conative and affective abilities. Teacher-education programmes are designed to prepare effective teachers by providing theoretical awareness of teaching and developing teaching competency and teaching ability.

The present level of performance of an individual on a test will indicate the growth of his ability.

Teacher-education covers those theoretical aspects through which knowledge, pertaining to specific subjects and transmitted to students and teachers, is prospected.

All those activities, operations and event through which the prospective teachers are to be made aware to the latest trends of subjects and teaching as well as pertaining to the theory related to learner's behavioural changes and behavioural management as well as subjecting them to situations—formal, and informal dealing to the development of communication of teaching skills. Finally, teacher-education is provided to prospective teachers consequent to which they develop interest in teaching.

The purpose of education is not only to acquaint him with certain skills and abilities but also developing his interest in teaching is necessary. Because if a teacher is interested he will continue to acquire new knowledge and shall put better and still better.

Teaching goes in the class with the intention that his students will learn something. For this purpose planning is required that is done with the help of mind *i.e.*, central nervous systems. Planning is based on certain rules, planning analysis, planning teaching learning activities and evaluation. Teacher through his mind prepare a theoretical hypothetical model which is translated in the class. Motivational activities are done so that the students are interested. The result is the student's behaviour. Now the student's behaviour is changed. If the students have learned there will be feedback to the students. If the teacher is dissatisfied with his teaching there will be not a change in teacher's perception and he has to change his strategy. But if he is satisfied there will be confirmation to his activities and lie will try to employ the same strategy in his further teaching. We have to learn that best can help our students to learn. What are these teaching practice and strategies, which should be in a successful teaching?

In all teacher-education theory, curriculum as well as practical curriculum, there are objectives. To achieve these objectives there are certain programmes. Teacher is assigned some course to teach. Schedule for a activities prepared. In planning it is not merely the case to help the student-teacher to plan his lesson but to help him to become an educator.

Through particular experience the S.T. is helped to know the role of educator.

This is the cooperation plan of teacher-education (T.E.) as well as Student-teaching (S.T.). It will deliver the plan in the class and the T.E. will supervise the S.T. As the teacher-educator will see whatever the student-teacher has developed the desired skills or not, it will give him feedback, while, the student-teacher will see whether his students have learnt.

Teacher-education refers to all those programmes, strategies tactics as a result of which a prospective teacher is able to help his students to acquire learning-cognitive psychomotor and affective.

The following are the general objectives of teacher education programmes:

1. Teacher-education has the general objectives of develop Gandhian values of non-violence, truthfulness, self-discipline, self-reliance and dignity of labour.
2. Not only acts as a leader of the student community but also as guide to the wider community.
3. Perceives the role as an agent of social change in the community.
4. Not only uses but also helps in the conservation of environmental resources and life and preservation of historical emoluments and other cultural heritage.
5. Established a liaison between the school and the community by employing ways and means for integrating the resources as a life of the community with school life.
6. Develops an understanding of the objectives of student-teaching in the Indian context and awareness

of the role played by school in achieving the goals of developing a democratic, secular and socialistic society.

7. Develops a warm and positive attitude towards the growing children their academic socio-emotional and personal problems.
8. Develops competency to teaching on the basis of accepted principles of learning and teaching.
9. Develops understandings, interests, attitudes and skills which will enable him to foster the all round growth and development of the children under his care.
10. Develops communication, psychomotor skills and abilities conducive for human relations which will enable him to promote learning inside and outside the classroom.
11. Keeps abreast with the latest trends in the knowledge of the subject he teaches and the techniques of teaching the same.
12. Undertakes investigations and action research projects.

Different Stages

The following are the basic assumptions for the objectives and teacher-education:

1. Since the objective of education is to build a man who can help in the development of a secular, democratic and socialistic society. Therefore, teacher-education must ensure the man-making process.
2. The continuity aspect of teacher implies that teacher-education should have a core curriculum. The core curriculum will be called to all the teacher-education

namely pre-primary, primary, seconuary and college level.

3. The diversity aspect of teacher-education programme implies that teacher-education. programme for each needs stage be designed in the context of children's developmental and national goals.

3. The man-making process is start right from infancy to adulthood, therefore, all levels of teacher-education will help to develop such teacher-education in which ensures continuity on the one hand and diversity in terms of the learners' characteristics and social demands.

5. Teacher-education programme of each stage should merge into a teacher-education programme of higher stage in the progressive order.

6. All teacher-education programmes irrespective of difference teacher-education levels should have the following three integral components:

   (a) Pedagogical course.

   (b) Working with the community.

   (c) Content-cum-methodology course and practice-teaching courses.

7. The pedagogical components working with community component and content of methodology component will vary in their proportionate weightage from stage to stage in the total teacher-education programme.

8. The three components stated above should form the nucleus of teacher-education for reasons as under:

   (a) The prospective teacher must be familiarized with the work why and how of teacher

behaviours, the answer to these questions have to be supplied to him on the basis of accepted principles of pedagogy, psychology and sociology.

(b) The prospective teacher will have to be a matter over the subject and an expert in the teaching methodology of the subject of his teaching.

(c) The prospective teacher must be an agent of social change, leader of the students and guide to the society.

9. Consequent to the integral components of teacher-education the prospective teacher will act inside and outside the classroom situation on the basis of scientific knowledge, positive attitude and convictions he will apply those techniques of modifying and managing learning behaviours which will be of use in actualizing learners's potentials.

10. To be effective, a teacher needs to have a close understanding of the characteristics of the society, of the community in which he lives and also be equipped with social skills through which he may help in community development and desirable social change.

11. Teacher-education being an on-going process needs to have three basic characteristics, namely flexibility, relevance and inter-disciplinary.

12. Teacher-education programme will be valid to the extent oral experiences are reinforced by visual, factual and motor experiences.

    The teacher-education programme therefore needs to be vivid, varied and comprehensive.

13. Teacher-education programme should, embrace two types of courses namely content or subject courses

and method courses. The content courses should including learning experience pertaining to the subject of teaching the teacher after completion of training is expected to teach. The method courses should impart knowledge and help in the development of two types of skills.

(a) Core teaching skills common to all stages of teacher-education.

(b) Specific teaching skill meant for a specific group of teachers at a specific level of teacher-education pre-primary primary, secondary and collegiate.

(c) Theory course should be drastically cut to include only suck theoretical concepts as are of significance in the understanding of the learner and in the modification of his cognitive, psychomotor and effective behaviour.

Education at Pre-primary Stage

It has been assumed that, teacher who will be educated in the pre-primary teacher institution, will generally teach children between 3 to 8 years of age. This age group is considered psychologically to be the most important formulated years of an individual's life span.

Freud believed that foundations of personality of an individual are made in the first five years of his age. This being so, teacher at pre-primary level need to be the best equipped in terms of his ability to help in laying, down strong foundation for a normal human personality and also the competencies which may enable him to actualize an individual's inherent potentials.

However, little care in the country till date has been made in designing a teacher-education curriculum which may develop knowledge, skills and attitudes among the prospective teachers to help in the personality building process as well as in naturalisation of young children's potentials.

National Council of Educational Research and Training (NCERT) broucher has laid down the following objectives of teacher-education at pre-primary stage:

1. Acquires theoretical and practical knowledge of childhood education.
2. Applies theoretical and practical knowledge to the education of the, children in Indian context-rural, urban an industrial.
3. Understands the major principles of growth and development of the children.
4. Develops understanding, skills, attitudes and interests which will enable him to foster all round growth and development of the children under his care.
5. Develops skills to help in the physical and emotional health of the children by providing a conducive environment.
6. Develops skills to provide a variety of learning experiences through organization of musical, rhythmic grammatic activities, play, worth experience, creative art and games.
7. Develops communication skills such as story telling explaining situations, etc.
8. Develops skills to provide visual aids with the help to waste of indigenous material.
9. Understands the role of the school and the teacher in changing the society.

10. Understands the home environment of the child and develops amicable home-school relationship.

Education at Primary Stage

The learner at the primary stage has a better developed cognitive, psychomotor and affective abilities. He has a better capacity in comparison to the learner at the pre-primary stage to make abstractions, to think, to reason out, to draw inference, to manipulate words, to communicate, to develop proper relationship with peers, social group, home, neighbourhood and the society to conform to social norms, to control his emotions and express his feelings. Consequent these developments and also according to social expectations' because of origin of new problems, new perspectives, new dimensions, in his life the teacher's talk at this stage is no less crucial and significant than what it was during pre-primary stage. To be successful as a teacher, the prospective teacher should acquire, the following behavioural changes:

1. Possesses knowledge of the first and second, language topics related to social and natural sciences related to environmental studies.
2. Possesses theoretical and practical knowledge in respect of the child's health, physical and creational activities, work experiences, play, games creative art and music and the skills to conduct these activities.
3. Develops skills to identify, select and organize learning experiences pertaining to subjects and also the skills to conduct them.
4. Develops understanding of the major psychological principles pertaining to growth and development of the children under his care.
5. Develops, understanding of the major principles of learning in formal and informal situations.

6. Possesses theoretical and practical knowledge in respect of childhood education including integrated teacher.

7. Understands the role of the school and teacher in changing the society.

8. Understands the role of the school, the peer group and the community in shaping the personality of the child and also develops an amicable home school relationship.

Education at Secondary Stage

The following are the basis for the objectives:

1. The child is at the adolescent stage and has problems.
2. All mechanism of growth and development.
3. Child, after the completion of adolescence, is ready to choose vocation and pursue it upto his optimum level.
4. Child's interests at this stage become crystallized in their interaction with varied situation.
5. Child's interests in religion, society, politics, nation and work at large trends to be manifested.

11

School Discipline and Punishment

The concept of discipline is viewed in two ways. From a narrower and older point of view discipline means order among school students and involves subjection to school authority, obedience to laws framed by the school administrator, maintenance of law and order among students and in the school, and lastly, imposition of disciplinary measures for disobedience of any form or any kind. This form of discipline lays stress on perfect control by authority, total subjection to rules, complete obedience to law and order, strict observance of rules and regulations. Under such a form of discipline, there is pindrop silence in the classroom, a calm and quiet atmosphere in the school, an utter absence of noise or disturbance of any kind. This narrow concept confuses discipline with school order.

Discipline and Order Contrasted. Order consists in the acceptance of external authority; discipline, in the submission of one's impulses to a regulation, which brings efficiency and economy in place of chaos, inefficiency and waste. Herbart used two different terms : Zuchet for discipline and Regierung for order. By 'Zuchet' he meant the whole influence of the school in the child *i.e.,* character training. By Regierung he meant behaviour of the child in the school.

When there is an order in the school, the school work goes on smoothly and efficiently. Order is the maintenance of quietness. Order is the banishment of all signs of disrespect. for the teacher. When school order is bad we say school discipline is loose; but when school order is good it does not imply that discipline is also good. Discipline is not an external thing like order. It lies in the submission of one's impulses to a regulation which one imposes upon oneself. It is individual self-discipline.

Good order is sometimes mistaken for good discipline as we have already stated above. But it is nothing more than a cover for indiscipline, because we have sometimes great turmoil under calm surfaces. A good order in that case may be bad discipline: but a good discipline is always a good order. Good order is good government : good discipline is good training. Good order is a condition where traces of disrespect to the school authorities are totally banished whereas good discipline is a condition where the student chooses the right course of action and discards the wrong one.

Modern Concept

The modern concept of discipline as indicated above implies submission of one's impulses to regulation which one imposes upon oneself. In this sense it is something internal and may be regarded as a response to an inner stimulus. It implies not only bringing under control, but also submitting one's instructive tendencies to self-imposed regulations. The individual, who controls his own behaviour, willingly and spontaneously identifies himself with what is right. Self-control means self-discipline.

True Discipline is Self-discipline

Where the individual chooses the right and discards the wrong course of action, where the person selects the desirable rather than the opposite, and where he picks up the socially approved behaviour rather than the disapproved one there is true discipline. When scboolstudents are so trained that they can discriminate between what is good and what is bad, between what is right and what is wrong, and can adopt the good or right course of action without being controlled from above, we say that school discipline is good.

Authoritarian *Vs.* Democratic Discipline

True discipline is not authoritarian discipline which means control of the action of students by an individual with greater power. "The person with power decides what he wants done, how he wants it done and when he wants it done, and then forces others to carry out his purposes and plans. As he becomes sure of willingness and ability of others to execute what he wants done, he gives them greater freedom to plan and act within the framework of his purposes." In a school run by an authoritarian type of administration we have such a discipline. The authoritarian headmaster imposes control upon the students and teachers. He regulates their action through fear or respect. If he uses punishment as a means he is a dictatorial autocrat: if he uses respect as a means of imposing regulation, he is a benevolent autocrat. He is a leader with 'power over'. Students and teachers are afraid of either being punished for not carrying out his orders or they respect him so much that they will not think of disobeying his wishes. Discipline under such circumstances is not true discipline.

Conditions for Self-Discipline

Self-discipline in a school is true discipline. Conditions for self-discipline to grow are:

(a) A common purpose sufficiently strong to control the action of the individual.

(b) A clear conception of functions to be performed by each member of the group.

(*c*) A compelling desire to achieve that purpose and willingness to take up a common enterprise.

(*d*) An agreement on the regulations to be imposed on the group.

Self-discipline in the school can be developed most effectively when students are given enough chances of sharing responsibility and planning of school activities on a cooperative basis. It grows and develops in a democracy. The teacher or the Principal exercises his power only when he must. He does not dictate or command. He simply helps and guides. The democratic leader helps the children to understand school problems, to examine the various issues, to arrive at a decision and to execute it. He exercises 'power with' the group. He carries his students along with him. Whereas the authoritarian leader makes mere automatons of his students, the democratic leader creates human beings capable of sharing responsibilities.

Student Council

Good's dictionary defines student council as an organization for maintaining order and for regulation of matters of conduct in the school by the representatives chosen from the student body by students themselves. It is thus an organization of student's which gives them a chance to learn the skill of electing their leader and conducting their deliberation on democratic lines. In this way they get an ample scope for self-expression, evaluation and judgement.

A student council takes various forms. The simplest ones are Bal Sabha and House System. The Secondary Education Commission recommends the formation of the latter in each school because of its simplicity and practicability. The student body elects its own prefects or representatives and the whole school is divided into 4 or 5 houses which look after the school affairs.

Objectives

The objectives of a student council are:

(i) To develop harmonious relations between students and staff.

(ii) To promote student activity.

(iii) To assist in the management of the school.

(iv) To promote the welfare of the school.

(v) To develop attitudes of good citizenship.

(vi) To develop student initiative and responsibility.

(vii) To provide a laboratory for citizenship.

(viii) To provide an opportunity for the training of student leaders.

(ix) To provide a forum for the expression of students' grievances.

Principles of Organizing Student Councils

A student council is an organization of students elected by the students to represent them and to speak for them in many activities of the school. If it is to succeed, some principles should be kept in mind. These principles are:

1. **It should not be Imposed upon the Students.** They themselves should feel the necessity of forming an organization. Such a need arises when students do not attend the morning assembly either because they have not come in school uniform or because they have not cared for personal cleanliness. When there is soch a concrete problem before them to solve, they should be led to form a committee for supervising the morning assembly.

2. **The Organization should Grow Gradually.** If students are playing truant from the assembly, a small class organization

may be formed in the shape of a small committee to handle the problem. It *is* always wise to form a small council and then let it grow big.

3. **It should have definite powers** and duties specified in its constitution.

4. **The Organization should not be too Large.** An executive committee be formed if the membership grows big.

Special Features

A good student council has the following special features.

1. It has clearly defined powers and responsibilities.
2. It gets it support from the staff and the Headmaster.
3. It is democratically organized and its constitution and by laws are formed democratically.
4. It enlists the ready and willing cooperation of the student body.
5. Its organization is sound and it functions well.

SELF-GOVERNMENT THROUGH STUDENT COUNCILS

The schools is a group and disciplinary control of group members by each other is a necessity. Individual students may be self-disciplined and able to control their behaviour but as a group they may still display anarchistic tendencies and it so happens in schools generally. A child may be self-disciplined but when he is in the group he becomes indisciplined. Self-discipline by individuals is not enough. The administrator is confronted with the task of maintaining discipline in the school. If the school is to function well, the students should impose discipline on themselves. The students should as members of the school accept common, purposes and feel their strength.

Need of Student Self-government. In olden days, when the Headmaster was the absolute monarch of the school, the school government was authoritarian and was conducted wholly by the Headmaster only. With the growth of the number of students and teachers, the Headmaster began to share the responsibility of governing the school affairs with the help of his assistants. During teachers' absence, the duty of maintaining order in the class was handed over to the monitors or prefects. Now when most of the countries of the world have adopted democracy as a form of government, the complexion of school government has also changed. The adult society now wants its children to be trained in democratic principles and requires from the schools that they should provide to the children as many opportunities as possible for teaching them democratic ways of life.

Schools now have begin to give ample opportunities to the children to govern themselves. Social and civic responsibilities are given to them, and training is given to make them better citizens. They are made to realise that they have a common purpose, a common interest, and a common destiny with the Principal and teachers.

Conditions for Self-discipline

Group self-discipline exists when the group has common purposes sufficiently to control the actions of individual members. It is therefore the responsibility of the teachers and the Principals to lead their students to accept common purpose. A disciplined student would then be one who has a clear understading of the goals of the school and a compelling desire to achieve them by working with, in, and for the school. Students should accept responsibility voluntarily. They should agree on the rules necessary for attaining the purposes set by the school. They is how they can achieve group self-discipline.

Nothing is more important for developing a sense of group self-discipline than the enforcement of rules arrived at by common decision by the students themselves. Under the scheme of authoritarian discipline imposed by the teachers or headmasters, the control is from above and it is capable of regulating students' actions through the power of fear or respect. Either the students must be afraid that they will be punished for not carrying out the orders of the Principal or they must respect him so much that they will not think of disobeying his wishes. This is dictatorial control.

If students themselves through their councils select their leaders democratically and decide proper codes of conduct and give them the responsibility of getting the rules observed it would lead to group self-discipline. Student-government of this type would lead to the maintenance of order and regulation of conduct in the school. The main responsibility would then rest on the shoulders of the student leaders selected by the students body itself and discipline will be better.

Different countries have experimented with five different forms of student governments:

1. Specific Service Type. Students in the form of government are given responsibilities permanently for specific services. They are completely in charge of these services, for example, cleanliness of the school.

2. The Informal Type. This is a temporary organization in which the senior students are given specific responsibilities, like those of receiving guests, decorating halls, looking after cleanliness of the school premises.

3. The Complex Type. There are more councils than one. A small body of school students representatives looks after the executive, functions: the bigger body keeps the legislative powers with it.

4. Simple Council Type. The whole student body elects members to look after the broad aspects of the school, for example, cleanliness, decoration, publication of magazines etc. The central council is responsible to the Principal.

5. The School City Type. Just as in a city we have Councillors and the Mayor, so also in a school different groups are formed akin to wards. These groups select their councillors. The Municipal councillors in the school elect the school Mayor, who is the head of the city government. The council has judicial and legislative powers. Standing committees look after finance, publications, social welfare, athletics, and other businesses.

In India, we can adopt the Simple Council Type. Such a system of student government is known as the House System or the Bal Sabha.

Bal Sabha. Bal Sabha or House System is a type of student council and has five (or more) boards whose members are selected from the elected representatives of the different classes in the school. The functions of these boards are:

1. *Management of games and sports*—arranging of school tournament, organization of excursions and trips, care of the school garden.

2. *Health and sanitation of school premises*—cleanliness of school building, playgrounds, classrooms, decoration of the school building, organization of lunch room and cafeteria, organization of health services, supervision of ventilation and light arrangements.

3. *Organization of cultural activities* like debates, dramas and wall magazines, organization of contests and competitions, promotion of good behaviour in the assemblies and functions and public meetings, organization of exhibitions, arrangement of lectures.

4. *Social service activities* like literary campaigns, assistance in community drives.

5. *Disposal of cases* of indiscipline among students.

The Boards get their strength from class committees. In each class there is a committee of five members, *i.e.,* as many members as there are boards. In any class there are members of as many houses as the school authorities want to have in the Bal Sabha Programme. In the class there in one representative of each house and is elected by the members of that house in that class. The house committee is formed of the representatives of that house in different classes. All the house committees meet together and form the General House Committee. In each class committee, as stated before, we have a, member of the five boards listed as above.

The Bal Sabha is a means for training schoolstudents it the art of living together. For the successful working of Bal Sabha, responsibility should be delegated to the Boards or Houses and it is of no use if the Principal and the teachers are just round the corner to exercise their authority. Heavy responsibilities should be delegated to them as they grow in experience. All forms of student-governments require intelligent supervision which may not admit of too much indifference or too much control. A good student government imparts a wholesome social atmosphere and fosters common purposes. It imposes self-discipline on the student group. It trains the student personnel in citizenship and democratic way of life.

Students learn self-control not by hearing, but by practising it. Bal Sabha gives an opportunity to them to practise self-control or group self-discipline. In a democratic setup of the school, students should be induced to learn how to govern themselves, how to take the initiative, how to judge and criticise themselves. how to weigh pros and cons and come to a decision and how to observe self-made laws and rules. A system of self-government makes them see the reasonableness of rules. They understand rules better, what they are for and why they have been framed. They realise that as these rules are made by themselves they must obey them. Self-discipline is thus a better type of discipline than the one imposed from above by the Principal.

Limitations and Difficulties of Student Self-government

If a system of self-government is adopted in a school. it does not mean that it will be able to solve all disciplinary problems. As a matter of fact, it is a more difficult device to establish discipline in the school than the authoritarian form of discipline imposed from above by means of a series of orders and commands. Difficult though it is, yet it is a surer method of establishing and maintaining discipline.

Difficulties in the Way of Self-government

The following are the difficulties:

1. The Principals and teachers do not like to share authority with the students. They do not want to part with power rather. Their prestige becomes in danger. As the students have little experience of shaling authority and power with the teachers and the Principal, they behave sometimes. in a way which is irksome to the teachers.

But this difficulty even though real, can be faced by keeping patience till students get accustomed to such a system. Wherever the authority has been shared with students they have tended to create troubles. This is a real danger.

2. Because of lack of good relationship between students and teachers student councils have failed in achieving their objectives. Some teachers have been observed even actively opposing self-government. In some schools students councils exist in name only and the real power lies in the hands of teachers and the Head. The office-bearers are mere tools in

the hands of the teacher and the Head. They accept their opinions and impress them upon the fellow students. It is no use introducing such a system of student self-government where power lies elsewhere. Real power has to be given to students in the right spirit.

3. The student committees, which are responsible for establishing and maintaining discipline in the school, often err on the side of severity in inflicting punishment on the wrongdoers. The result is that the Headmaster has to watch them closely and refer their decisions back to the committee. With more experience the difficulty may be overcome.

4. Teachers and Headmaster do not allow students to carry out decisions even when they have jointly made them because their decisions, they fear, might go against the interest of the school.

5. The student councils are generally regarded as discipline committees and other functions, for example, cleanliness of premises, cultural activities etc., are neglected.

6. Senior students do not like to take office and share responsibilities because they fear that much of their time would be consumed in extra-curricular activities. They should be encouraged to participate to the maximum by telling them that school learning does not simply mean learning certain school subjects, but it also includes training for life.

7. Sometimes the President of the General Committee is wrongly elected by the student body. If elections are done every term, such inefficient office-bearers automatically move out of office and students also learn how to make good elections. Principals should in no case override an election because then the very spirit of democracy will be lost.

8. The General Committee becomes very unwiedly in case of very big schools. If work can be found for all, this difficulty is reduced.

9. A system of self-government cannot be worked with all teachers and all Principals. It requires certain qualities which all of us do not possess.

10. Sometimes the work of certain committee slackens. It is because children do not understand their responsibilities. If they are supervised closely then the difficuhy may be solved.

When a system of self-government is introduced in a school for the first time such difficulties do arise but the school authorities should not be discouraged and try the experiment whole-heartedly with necessary tact, perseverance and patience all the difficulties can be surmounted and students self-government may be made a success.

Some educationists feel that since experiments "in student self-government have not met with a success and since the difficulties cannot be surmounted by an average Principal, it is held that a broad students' participation may be adopted. Under this programme students are given opportunities to participate in the school management with teachers and the Principal as their guides. This appears to be a better way of maintaining school order and checking indiscipline among them.

Rewards and Discipline

Students are stimulated through rewards for good progress in studies, for efficiency in sports, games and cultural activities. Prizes are offered to them for showing good conduct, regularity of attendance, punctuality, honesty and other traits of moral behaviour. Rewards and prizes given to students in schools take the following forms:

1. Books and stationery articles of daily use.
2. Badges and merit certificates.
3. Shields and medals.

4. Praise and approval in assemblies.
5. Positions on the honour board.

The objective behind giving rewards to children is to motivate their behaviour in desired directions. Prizes and books are, for example, given to children who are meritorious in school work. Not only do we expect these children to show better results, but we wish that other children also should work harder.

But prizes are poor incentives. They are neither ethical. They may stimulate two or three top students but what about the remaining lot who remains the silent onlooker. It is not ethical also to reward a child who comes from a better home and is more privileged.

We should have given encouragement to one who inspite of his limitations works hard and may not get the top position.

Guiding Principles of Giving Rewards

The following principles are to be kept in mind when giving prizes and rewards to students for proficiency and good conduct.

1. Rewards should be given for sustained serious efforts only.
2. Prizes should be of small intrinsic value: those of high value create greed and competition among students. Flags, banners, and cups whose intrinsic worth is negligible should be given as rewards, because it is not the value of the article given as prize, which counts. The object of giving rewards is to stimulate interest and provide a motive for good work and good conduct.
3. Prizes should be smail in number and should not be obtainable without hard work, otherwise they will lose their worth.

4. Prizes should be given to groups and not individuals. To check unhealthy rivalry between individual members, and to promote group feeling among students, groups should be stimulated.

5. Prizes to individuals can, however, be given in case of individual triumphs; for example, when a student stands first in the class, or in the running track events he has to be rewarded for his individual worth.

6. Certificates should be given for gvod work and conduct because being of small instrinsic value they can be multiplied and can cover a large number of students. Some educationists and psychologists do not believe in the efficacy of giving prizes for good conduct. Conduct is not good when it is the result of bribery.

7. Prizes may also be given for minor virtues like punctuality, regularity of attendance, personal cleanliness and good behaviour.

Values of Rewards in Creating Discipline

Different and divergent views are held by schoolmasters as regards the usefulness of giving rewards to students for the maintenance of law and order in the school, or for improving class results or for raising the level of proficiency in games and sports. Naturalistic philosophy holds that rewards demoralise the person who gets them because they simply tempt him to show good work. The person then works for the sake of getting a prize and not for the sake of doing his duty. Rewards develop feelings of rivalry and unhealthy competition and students indulge in bad practices only for the sake of getting a reward.

Others believe that rewards and prizes work as incentives for good behaviour in the school. They motivate children to work harder at studies and show good behaviour. Rivalry also is a sort of motivation to excel. Rewards develop confidence in the individual students and they are encouraged to put more and more effort in school activities and to remain discipline.

Punishments and Discipline

Punishments are given as a disciplinary measure with an assumption that the individual will show good conduct out of fear for being punished. The following form of disciplinary measures are taken to improve child behaviour in schools.

1. Reproof. The tongue is the most powerful weapon in the teacher's armoury. Reproof means use of tongue to correct the child's behaviour. It takes different forms. It is mild. But when it becomes bitler, it takes the form of sarcasm and vulgar abuse. The self respect of the child is lowered (if the child is sensitive) even with a mild remark. The harsh sarcasm or rebuke becomes harmful. Hence, reproof is never an effective means of correcting or reforming the child's behaviour and should be sparingly used.

2. Detention during the Break. When a child does his work carelessly or does not do it at all, the common practice is to make him do it in the recess or redo it if it had been done carelessly with perhaps a little extra work also. Detention is disagreeable to students because it deprives them of the rest or recreation which they could get in the recess. Detention is disagreeable to teachers also for the same reason. Detention should be used only for negligence in work and not for mis-conduct because there is no connection between a crime and detention. Detention is simply meant for making up the loss. The lenght of period for which a child is detained should not be too great. A proper register should be maintained to show the names of children detained, the time for which they are detained, and the amount of work done. Teachers who are made in charge of this detention period should rotate.

3. Fines. Fines may be imposed on children who have attained the age of 14 years in the following cases:

1. Late attendance—a fine of 5 rupees per late attendance.
2. Absence from the class without obtaining permission from the Principal. The permission is to be granted on the application of the parent or guardian.
3. Truancy—running away from the class.
4. Wilful damage to school property.
5. Delay in payment of school fees and dues.

The amount of fine imposed depends upon the nature of offence committed. As fines are a burden on parents they should be imposed only when nothing else can be done. As there is no way out in certain cases referred to above, their imposition becomes a necessary evil. But something can be done to reduce the burden on the parent. For example, when a child has wilfully broken school furniture or damaged school property, he may be required to do some work on the school premises by doing which he may be able to meet the expenditure involved in making good the damage. Absence without leave is a fault of parents and they should not object to the imposition of absence fines. Late coming is a fault of the student and fine for late coming becomes justified because it has its effect when the parent reacts to it. If it is established that the student is responsible for absence from the school or for late coming, some other proper way to punish him should be adopted: in no case he should be let off by asking him to put in extra hour of study which he has skipped due to his absence in the school.

4. Rustication. Rustication means sending down a student temporarily from the school as punishment. But this punishment can be awarded only when the misdemeanour committed by him or her is of serious nature and the sanction for the punishment has been obtained from the Education Office : it is to be awarded when all other ways of punishment have been exhausted.

5. Suspension. We suspend a child for some serious misconduct and hope that no other way exists to reform him. We suspend him also because we want to protect other children from getting conteminated and helping the teacher in carrying on his normal work. The students is deprived of school company and is obliged to think and reform himself. This is a reformative type of punishment.

Value of Punishment

As in the case of rewards, so in the case of punishments different theories are held. There are educationists and philosophers who protest against any kind of punishment while there are educationists who believe in the values of disciplinary measures listed above. Rousseau says, "Children should never receive punishment as such—it should come as natural consequence of their fault." Herbert Spencer also holds a similar view and believes in the efficacy of natural consequences for the conduct shown by the child. Nunn says that punishment is merely a barbarous superstition. These philosophers believe in the greater fruitful effect of unwritten moral code of an institution which imposes rules of conduct from within.

Contrary views are held by a number of educationists. They say that punishment is like a surgical operation which removes the undesirable traits. It sets an example for others so that they may not commit the same kind of misdemeanour. For example, we fine a child who comes late with a view to reforming him as well as with an aim to set an example for others so that they may not come late. Bray regards punishment as lesser evil so that the greater one that exists in the future may be avoided. Some educationists belonging to this school do not regard punishment as vengeance or retribution. They take a positive and corrective view of punishment and regard it a useful measure of reformation.

Punishment and fear of punishment are useful in preventing students from doing something which adults do not think desirable. Fear of punishment may be expected to help in breaking bad habits. But it is of little value in creating good habits or developing a desire for active and constructive work. The effect of fear of punishment is generally negative. Punishment and fear of punishment are effective tools in the hands of an authoritarian administrator.

No school can hope to become an educational community if its teachers have a stiff forbidding attitude towards their students and try to maintain discipline through imposing various kinds of punishment while students stand in fear of them, and are not prepared to share their problems and difficulties with them.

'Spare the rod and spoil the child' is a maxim of those who believe in the usefulness of punishment for maintaining discipline. They hold that unrestricted freedom should not be given to children. A child is not a mature being and he is not to be given a long rope with which he may hang himself. Absolute freedom is not useful. They feel that law is absolutely necessary and restrictions are equally beneficial. On the other hand there are those who say, excessive restrictions are equally bad. The child confronted with do's and don'ts of the adult world gets his personality development checked. There is a mental paralysis.

"The man whose tongue is constricted by laws and taboos against free speech, whose pen is constricted by the censorship, whose laws are constricted by ethics, whose childhood has been imprisoned in a code of manners, whose youth has been drilled in a cruel orthodoxy, will feel against the world that tampers him with the same rage that is felt by an infant whose arms and legs are held motionless". Such is the evil effect of too much restrictions according to Russell.

The days, when rod was the chief instrument of keeping the child under control, has gone. Repression is now deemed to be dangerous. Under repressive regime the child becomes orderly only externally : but internally he is frustrated, militant, and rebellious.

Rationale Behind Inflicting Punishment

Why is a child fined for coming late? Why is he rebuked for not doing his home work? Why does he get his ears boxed when he commits a spelling mistake? Why is he caned in the assembly when he bas misbehaved with his class fellow seriously? He is fined because it is a rule and we want that rules should not be broken. His ears are boxed so that he may not make the spelling mistake again. He is caned so that he may not harm others and an example may be set before others. Thus punishment in schools is considered to be serving the following purposes.

1. Retaliating the Wrong Doer. 'An eye for an eye and a tooth for a tooth' goes the old saying. If the offender has done a wrong, the wrong must be avenged. For example, if the student has seriously misbehaved with a teacher, the misbehaviour must be avenged. If that is the motive behind punishment it is certainly a selfish motive and such punishment cannot be justified.

2. Protecting others from Further Wrong. A vicious dog is chained so that he may not bite others. A child who has misbehaved seriously with his class fellow is caned so that he may not do any further wrong to his fellow students and other students may be saved from further harm at his hands.

But will he certainly not commit the same wrong again? Does a dog become less vicious by being chained? If not, the punishment inflicted has no proper justification.

3. Vindicating the Rules and Regulations Violated. It is a rule made by the school that children should come to school in school uniform. If a child does not attend school in proper dress, he is rebuked and sent home. The Principal wants that his children should realize that school rules are rules and they should be strictly obeyed. If rules are violated, the offender will be punished. The motive behind such punishment lies in vindicating the rule violated.

But are not rules made for the convenience of school? Does not a school exist for the child? If so, such a punishment for vindicating the violation of rules of the school is not a proper thing. The reasons behind violation must be sought and then an action should be taken against the student.

4. Reforming the Wrong Doer. The only one good purpose served by punishment lies in making the wrongdoer realize that he has done a wrong and it was wrong to have done a wrong. It he feels sorry for what he has done he will buildup a positive attitude of mind and behave in a more disciplined manner in future.

5. Setting an Example to Reforms Others. We impose fines on a student who damages school property and set an example before other students so that they may reform themselves. We beat a child for truancy so that an example may be set before others that if they run away they shall meet the same fate. But is it fair to punish one to set an example before others so that they may reform themselves?

Indiscipline a Result of Bad School Organization

Behaviour is not born. It is caused. An undesirable behaviour is produced under certain conditions. For example, a child, who is running away from the school in the school time without the permission of the Principal and loafs outside, does not find the school environment pleasant. The causes of undesirable behaviour should be, therefore, scrutinized to determine whether it can be improved by modifying the nature of the school environment before inflicting fines for truancy. The Principal may attempt to force the child into a pattern of conduct demanded by the school. He may gain control over him through fear of punishment or through lure of rewards. But the real solution of the problem will have to be sought elsewhere He will have to realise that "it is his faulty or inadequate school organization that is responsible for many of the disciplinary problems.

Causes of School Indiscipline

A few examples will show how problems of undesirable behaviour are caused by inadequate or faulty school organization.

1. **An Unsympathetic Teaching Staff.** Such teachers make arbitrary and extravagant demands for exacting obedience and create behavioural problems that are uncommonly hard to solve.

2. **Inability to Create Challenging Situations.** The able child can frequently get into mischief because the organizational framework has prevented all his teachers from understanding the extent of his abilities. It is very harmful when we are not able to create, challenging learning situations in the classroom commensurate with his abilities.

3. **Academic Fustrations** and disappointments and failures are caused by non-promotion policies of the schools.

4. **School organization,** which requires a minimum standard of achievement in all subjects, creates difficulties for the child who is rejected by good students.

5. **The Lack of Cocurricular Activities and Organized Games** in a school leads children into undesirable modes of expressing their feelings.

6. **Heavy Assignments** from some teachers, none of whom know what other teachers are expecting may cause in young students tension.

7. **Inadequate, Unsuitable Classroom Furniture,** or lack of light and ventilation in rooms causes undesirable behaviour on the part of school children.

8. **Lack of Adequate Facilities** in the school, *e.g.,* arrangement of fresh drinking water inside the school premises forces child to move out of school boundaries and loaf outside.

Common Forms of Indiscipline in Schools

Indisciplined behaviour occurs at two levels—at individual level and at group level. When a child is in the group, the group mind works and if the group is undesirable, he may be involved in the following forms of misbehaviour:

(a) aggression, fighting, quarrelling

(b) strikes and gang behaviour

(c) rowdyism

(d) truancy

But a child may show individual indisciplined behaviour when he scribbles and writes indecent and abusive language upon the walls and in the latrines and bath rooms, or when he/she tells a lie or is found cheating others, or when comes late to the school and violates school rules.

Common forms of Indisciplined Behaviour in Schools. The forms of indiscipline in schools are milder in form than those seen in colleges. They are :

1 Aggressive behaviours, bullying, teasing, beating, fighting, stoning.

2. Dishonest dealings—cheating and stealing.

3. Late coming.

4. Damaging school property removing fixtures, stealing electric bulbs, setting fire to furniture.

5. Not respecting the teachers.

6. Not doing home work.

7. Scribbling.

8. Using unfair means, cheating in the examinations.

12

Curriculum Development

Curriculum is one of the most commonly used words of educational jargon and one of the most poorly defined. It is given a most restricted definition by some, while others see it as all the educational experiences of a learner in the school environment, or as "something that happens to learners." Rather than waste time in a futile debate of the concept and definition, this chapter will deal with some of the societal and other sources of what occurs in schools, and then detail what it is that happens within the boxes which we label as subject areas.

Content of the Curriculum

Inlow suggests that there are three basic sources from which we draw the substance of what goes on in our schools: (1) the age-old disciplines, (2) the emerging disciplines, and (3) the contemporary world. Good gives the three sources as societal pressure, the learner, and the organized subject-matter itself.

One of the most important sources of curriculum and curricular change has been the knowledge explosion. Since it is manifestly impossible to teach everything there is to know, educators must select from among a growing number of options that which is most appropriate and important for a child to know. With the expansion of knowledge, the ability of students to think for themselves and act like scientists became important curricular objectives, in addition to the traditional mastery of information. Modern technology in the form of computers, machinery of all types, and the mass media have also had profound curricular implications, not only from the standpoint of the kinds of jobs for which the schools must prepare their students, but also in the way in which technology can be put to instructional use. Numerous other societal influences, such as the environmental crises issues of war and peace, life expectancy and other demographic factors, and economic factors of wealth and poverty, affect what happens to the child in the school setting.

Equally significant for curricular change and reform have been understanding about how and when children learn, ideas gleaned from developmental and educational psychologists. In such areas as physical, emotional, and social maturation and their effects on learning, much research has gone into the concept of student readiness. The research of Piaget has been most important in helping to develop appropriate materials for children in school, while the concepts of Maria Montessori have given additional impetus to the movement to provide students with tasks appropriate to their stage of development. Moving children from the specific and the concrete to the general and more abstract is another curricular principle taken from research on children's styles of learning.

Jerome Bruner in his book "The Process of Education" set forth most clearly the third major source of curricular decisions, namely the academic disciplines themselves. Numerous school subjects went through a dramatic reform the early as a result of Bruner and his colleagues' emphasis upon the disciplines in low lists the basic points made by the disciplinary theorists as follows:

1. Structure within each discipline consists of the fundamentals (and/or concepts, and/or powerful ideas) that are sequential and related.

2. Each discipline has its own unique structure.
3. Each discipline has its own methods and tools of discovery—sometimes discrete, sometimes shared with other disciplines.
4. Because mastery of copious detail is impossible and undersirable, details should be grouped into a structured pattern of concepts, formulas and theory from which non-specific as well as specific transfer may be made.
5. Teaching and learning should follow the methods that brought the discipline into being in the first place, and act, on a continuing basis, to refine its conceptualizations.
6. A discipline is never to be converted into a teaching arrangement; it is the teaching arrangement. It is to be learned as the scholars learned it and developed it.

In the mid 1970s the call had gone up for a return to the basics. Whether the curriculum is caught on a pendulum or goes through some type of cyclical reform movement is difficult to say, but, in the area of what should be taught and the methods for teaching it, there is a constant call for change and reform.

Many observes of curriculum at all levels have placed it on a continuum from subject-centered on the one extreme to learner-centred on the other extreme, with the one emphasizing content and the other process.

GOALS OF ELEMENTARY EDUCATION

Objectives

Education at the elementary level in colonial times was usually a function of the church and had as its basic purpose the salvation of the child from sin. With the development of mass education in the 19th century, social and economic objectives took primacy.

With the expansion of secondary education in the 20th century and the impact of such men as Edward L. Thorndike and John Dewey, elementary education began to change. It was no longer terminal for all students, and began to be looked upon as a preparatory institution for the high school. Thorndike took many of the ideas of psychology and applied them to the school situation, emphasizing such concepts as the importance of readiness in the child's ability to learn, and the transferability of learned material and behaviours from one situation to another. His stimulus-response theories led to greater emphasis upon drill. John Dewey, without doubt the greatest educator America has ever produced, had a profound impact on elementary education.

Language Arts. Without question, the dominant part of the curriculum in the primaly years is the area of language arts. With impetus both from federal programmes such as "Right to Read" and from the dissatisfaction of numerous parents, reading skills have taken on a new urgency in the elementary schools. The "return to the basics" movement and the establishment of numerous "fundamental" schools highlight the importance that parents and educators alike are placing on the basic language skills. Listening, writing, speaking, and spelling from other parts of the language arts curriculum.

The "New English," with its base in linguistics, the scientific study of language, has had a growing impact on the elementary school language arts curriculum. Transformational and descriptive grammar have replaced the more traditional forms, while creative writing, and a greater emphasis upon oral language, speaking, and listening, are among the trends found in the "New English." The teaching of English as a second or foreign language to children from homes, which use substandard English dialects is another aspect of the language arts programme in the elementary schools. For children who speak a black dialect at home, this has involved learning to not look down on their own "language," but to also master standard English as a tool to succeeding in the mainstream of society. In these programmes, children are taught initially in their native language and then are helped to gain facility in standard English. Children come to the schools with varying amounts of English-speaking ability, and the new programmes attempt to take the child were he or she is at, give them a pride and facility in their native language and culture, in addition to improving their skills in English.

Social Studies. Social studies in the elementary school developed out of the traditional disciplines of history and geography, and have expanded over the years to include parts of all the social sciences. Rather than take a disciplinary approach, the social studies have developed a pattern in which children move from an analysis of their home and school in the first grade, to the neighbourhood and city in the second and third grades, on to the state and nation in the fourth and fifth grades, concluding with a study of the world in the sixth grade. Although coming in for criticism from professional historians and social scientists, the social studies programme has for the most part been fairly well accepted by the public, until the past few years.

The elementary social studies were not immune to the efforts of social scientists to help children think like historians or economists and numerous curriculum materials were added to the elementary schools, bringing basic social science concepts down to the level of kindergartens. Approaches stressing inquiry have begun to replace the more traditional memorization of facts. Topics such as values, differing economic and political systems, and questions of social justice have begun to take their place alongside the "facts" of history.

Mathematics. Of all of the reforms in the curriculum, perhaps the "new math" has been the most threatening to both parents and teachers. Traditional mathematics education was based upon a stimulus-response theory of learning, and consisted of memorization, drill, and repetition. This type of programme gave way to a push for a rational understanding of what processes were being used in solving the problem, and finally to the "new math," which takes its lead, as did the other curricular reforms of the 1960s, from the structure of the discipline itself. Having been taught under the traditional system and having little understanding of the discipline, parents and teachers were slow in adopting the newer methods. Instead of the What? questions, the "new math" asks the Why? questions.

As with the shakedown period in any curricular reform, there were excesses during which children did not master the basic skills necessary for modem society. As a result, the "new math" came under attack, and in recent years, a new synthesis of the old and the new is developing, which will hopefully train young people in the basic computational skills of their parents' era, but also give them the basic understandings of the discipline, so necessary in our modern technological society.

Science. With the Russian space success in 1957, the United States moved into a new era in science education. The schools were looked upon as the cause for the United States' failure to beat the Russians into space, even though one educator stated that all that Sputnik proved was that "the Russians had more and better German scientists than we did." Regardless of the cause of Russia's space successes, they did have a demonstrable effect on the quality and quantity of input into elementary curriculum projects. Numerous "pure" scientists suddenly became interested in the schools, as federal funds poured into such groups as the Elementary School Science Project and many others like it.

Science teaching moved from the memorization of a few unrelated facts and the playing with animals in the classroom, to the serious business of helping children to understand the basic scientific concepts in each of the disciplines. Approaches to learning that stressed discovery replaced the more didactic classroom practices, and countless "hands-on" materials were brought into the classroom. In addition, children were taken out of the school to learn the concepts of ecology, biology, botany, astronomy, and other sciences, which can best be taught in the natural environment. Massive amounts of equipment were paid for with federal funds, and tens of thousands of teachers received training in special National Defense Education Act (NDEA) institutes. Inquiry or the scientific method forms the base of the elementary science curriculum today, but as was the case in mathematics, teachers have been slow to adopt new methods, and with the plethora of elementary science materials on the market today, it is still too early to state exactly where science in the elementary school is going.

Other Curricular Areas. The four areas dealt with so far from the academic core of the elementary curriculum, and because of their long history and strong public support, they will no doubt remain the core for generations to come. Physical education, art, and music are generally seen as peripheral activities in the curriculum of the elementary school. They are often taught by specialists, particularly in departmentalized intermediate programmes. As a result, when the budget crisis strikes, it is these "nonessential" programmes, which are often the first to be cut.

Every set of goals or purposes of elementary education gives lip service to the need for the physical and aesthetic development of the child, but at its core, the school curriculum is still academic in nature. Music teachers have recently begun a radio advertising campaign, using nationally famous musicians, to "educate" the public on the importance of "music in our schools." Without doubt, the education of our young is incomplete without physical and aesthetic education. Teachers in these programmes have begun to gain a "new" perspective on their role in the elementary school setting-perhaps just in time. Slowly, but surely, they have moved away from producing the star athlete or performer-musician, to a new and more relevant role of participant music and athletics for all students.

Curriculum in the Junior High School and Middle School

One of the most persuasive reasons for the replacement of the junior high school with the middle school is the traditional nature of the junior high school curriculum. If the colleges and universities of this country can be accused of dictating the curriculum for the high school, then the same charge can he levelled at the high school for the undue influence it has over the junior high school. The influence is not one of dictating entrance requirements. Rather, junior high school teachers, with few exceptions, are trained in the same manner as high school teachers, the textbooks are slightly watered-down versions of the high school texts, teaching methods are much the same, and the organization of classes tends to be similar. Even the name "junior" implies a slightly less-developed version of the high school. This is not to state that there are not some differences in the two institutions. Junior high schools are much more likely, at least at the seventh grade level, to have a block time programme, in which English and social studies are combined, along with a possible science mathematics block or some other combination of courses. This blocking of courses is defended on the grounds that the junior high school young people need more extended contact with one teacher, as was their elementary experience, and on the basis of a wide variety of justifications concerning the integration of subject matter. By ninth grade, however, block or core programmes have generally disappeared, and the curriculum closely resembles that of most high schools. In fact, Carnegie units from ninth grade courses are generally counted for admission to universities, and this leads to further control of the curriculum.

The organization of the school day parallels that of most senior high schools with six or seven fifty-minute periods, although some have moved towards modular scheduling and other innovations more common at the senior high level. Required courses make up most of the curriculum for most junior high students. Despite extensive lip service to individualized education, the greatest number of students take three years of English, social studies, mathematics, and science, with a few electives in the arts, vocational training, and foreign languages. Students are grouped by ability in a majority of junior high schools; this grouping begins the tracking process, which is accentuated at the senior high level.

In services and programmes provided as extracurricular activities, the junior high schools fall somewhere between the elementary schools and senior high schools. Guidance services are found in most junior high schools, with some of the guidance function being performed by a homeroom teacher. Clubs and sports, both intramural and interscholastic, are considerably more developed at the junior high school than at the elementary level. Critics see them as starting children too early in the "adult" competitive roles, social and athletic, and feel that young people in the midst of puberty don't need additional pressures placed on them by adult society.

Goals for Modern Secondary Education

Most of the attempts at improving on the Seven Cardinal Principles have explained in more detail what the secondary schools should do in the way of educating for citizenship, intellectual development, spiritual or ethical growth, vocational skills, and personal and interpersonal growth and skills. In the sixties and seventies of the last century one of the people most influential in the reform of secondary education has been James S. Coleman. In a Phi Deita Kappa article in December, 1972, he elaborated on the skills which every young person should have before the age of eighteen. He does not claim that they are all-inclusive, but does suggest that they must be explicitly included in the educational system.

1. Intellectual skills, the kinds of things that schooling at its best teaches.
2. Skills of some occupation that may be filled by a secondary school graduate, so that every eighteen-year-old would be accredited in some occupation whether he continued in school or not.
3. Decision-making skills; *i.e.,* those skills of making decisions in complex situations where consequences follow from the decisions.
4. General physical and mechanical skills, *i.e.,* skills allowing the young person to deal with physical and mechanical problems he will confront outside in work, in the home, or elsewhere.
5. Bureaucratic and organizational skills; *i.e.,* how to cope with a bureaucratic organization, as an employee, customer, or client, or as a manager or entrepreneur.
6. Skills in the care of dependent persons; *i.e.,* skill in caring for children, old persons, and sick persons.
7. Emergency skills; *i.e.,* how to act in an emergency or unfamiliar situation in sufficient time to deal with the emergency.
8. Verbal communication skills in argumentation and debate.

Coleman's suggestions are not unique, but they do tend to strike a note of reality, in the midest of so many lists of goals and purposes, which are so esoteric or abstract that the schools seldom change as the result.

The secondary school is a part of the society, and as such is often seen as part of the solution to problems confronting the society in general. Perhaps the greatest evidence of this is in the area of social class and caste, in which the schools through integration, programmes for the culturally different, and busing are being asked to bear the brunt of societal and cultural change. The same is true of the changes in technology. As the economy changes rapidly, the schools are expected to keep up by introducing new courses to prepare students for a future filled with change. When a breakdown of values appears in the society, the schools are asked to teach values, and when juvenile delinquency threatens the culture, the schools are asked to deal with the problem. When young people appear to be threatening democratic values as perceived by their elders, new curricula are added in an attempt to democratize youth. Schools traditionally reflect the society in which they find themselves. Although George Counts titled his provocative book are the Schools Build a New Social Order? The answer through the ages has been that the schools are not equipped to change very rapidly, much less to change the whole social order. The school must continue to confront the issues of the society, or the young people will continue to see many of its activities as irrelevant; but its ability to solve the massive problems of discrimination, values changes, economic deprivation, and lack of spiritual direction is questionable.

Secondary School Programme

In most high schools the programme is based on departmentalization, similar to that found at the university. As discussed in the previous section on the junior high school, departmentalization has come down from the university, all the way to the intermediate grades. Teachers are seen as specialists in one discipline, and knowledge tends to become compartmentalized for secondary students. Junior and senior high school young people see the world through the various disciplines, and come to expect that adults spend one hour each day "doing English," another "doing science," and on through the various subjects which are part of their schooling experience. Many experiments have been conducted on methods for breaking away from the traditional programme and curriculum, but compartmentalized knowledge, offered by specialists, in fifty-minute time blocks, to thirty or forty students, for which they receive one Carnegie unit of credit towards graduation and college entrance, and for which they receive a grade, still tends to dominate the secondary schools of the United States.

The correlated curriculum, in which attempts are made to relate one course to another, is one method for breaking down the discrete nature of the secondary school curriculum. The broad-fields approach to the curriculum combines the various social science disciplines into a social studies course, drawing concepts and approaches from each of the disciplines. The same approach can be used in a general science course or general business course. The core curriculum in its most radical form abolishes all disciplinary lines and has students working on the solutions to problems of an interdisciplinary nature. In its less radical form, it attempts to combine certain subject areas, and gives a teacher a larger block of time in which to get to know his or her students, and to stress social values, in addition to the traditional academic ones. The activity curriculum takes the student's needs and interests as its basis and structures the learning environment around them.

Another area of concern and controversy at the secondary level is the comprehensive versus the specialized high school. Comprehensive secondary schools serve the needs of a heterogeneous student population, while the specialized high schools, such as those found in the arts and sciences and the vast number of vocational schools throughout the country, serve a more homogenous population. The comprehensive secondary school has been justified as a more democratic institution and one that prevents the slotting or tracking of students. Its critics, however, state that within most comprehensive secondary schools, students are still tracked into college preparatory and vocationally-oriented programmes, and that prestige and status still tend to reside in the academically-oriented curricula.

On an instructional level many changes have been occurring in the secondary schools. The traditional lecture-recitation method still predominates in many classrooms, but with the vast amounts of new materials available as a result of the curriculum movement of the 1960s, most classrooms today have begun to move towards inquiry and discovery approaches to learning. Technology has also had its effect on the secondary school classroom, with programmemed materials now available in most subject areas, and highly sophisticated computer programmes being used in science and mathematics classrooms. Individualized materials have made it possible for the teacher to give more than lip-service to the goal of individualized instruction. Simulations and gaming techniques, first used in foreign policy and military decision-making, are now available in a variety of disciplines for use at the secondary level and are providing students with greater realism when it comes to social problems, business decisions, technological change, and the environment. Television and radio are being used, though not as extensively as had been hoped in the 1950s and 1960s. Closed circuit television can help to individualize instruction, show videotapes on demand, or perform many instructional services in the school. Television from an airplane or satellite is providing students in remote areas with many of the instructional benefits previously limited to large wealthy urban and sub-urban schools.

Of importance in the development of the American secondary school has been the growth of the extracurricular, co-curricular, or activities programmes. For many students these programmes are what keep them in school. Special-interest clubs, student publications, dramatics, debating societies, bands, choral groups, orchestras, athletic teams, and student government activities all go into making the secondary school much more than the sum of its formal learning programme. It is no wonder that guidance programmes are needed at the secondary level to aid young people in making career choices, deal with their sex role and relationships with the opposite sex, receive academic counselling, and just cope with an incredible overload. Critics of the high schools have suggested that they are part of the cause of juvenile delinquency and teenage suicides. It is certain true that the secondary student in most of our high schools does not lack for sensory input.

English-Language Arts

The language arts programme plays a central role in the secondary school curriculum, with a majority of school, requiring students to take English courses during each of their years in the senior high school. No area of the curriculum has come in for as much criticism as the English programme. Parents, college teachers, and employers all blame the schools for what they see to be vast numbers of illiterate or semiliterate young people graduating from secondary schools. Concern over the decline in college entrance scores has led many universities to institute "bonehead" English courses for some entering freshmen and has put pressure on the secondary schools to strengthen their programmes. If it is true that a large percentage of graduates from our high schools are functionally illiterate, it is equally true that English teachers are not the only ones to blame. Parents, television, changing values, and a host of unknown factors most also be included in the causes.

The language arts curriculum contains not only such basic skills as reading, writing, speaking, and listening, but has come to include such things as semantics, play production, public speaking, and the use of television, to name but a few of the many topics included in a high school study guide. It is the so-called frills which, critics of the secondary schools are demanding be dropped from the curriculum, but with the changing nature of modern society, it is difficult to state with any precision exactly what constitute the "basic skills" for the twenty-first century.

Attempts are being made to allocate certain skills and materials to specific grade levels, and to develop scope and sequence charts to aid teachers in dealing with the vast amounts of material without too much overlap. Reading, both remedial and developmental, is becoming an increasingly important part of the secondary school language arts programme Traditional prescriptive grammar is being replaced by descriptive structural approaches, although attacks are being made on the "new English." As with other areas of the curriculum, the language arts have moved towards discovery and inquiry approaches to learning, and the individualization of materials. The critical use of the mass media and the importance of oral expression have become increasingly important aspects of the modern language arts curriculum at the secondary level.

Social Studies and History

History, as an area of study, has suffered to such an extent that professional historians have called for its "re-introduction" into the schools. With economics, psychology, geography, anthropology, and a host of contemporary problems-oriented courses all vying for a place in the curriculum, history has slowly been shunted aside.

Traditional citizenship education and the study of history has given way to a discipline-oriented, inductive, problems-based approach to the social studies. The social studies have begun to deal in considerably greater depth with the study of values and value-related questions. This has been both welcomed by some of the public who see the school as needing to teach values, and opposed as one more attempt at the secularization of society and the taking away of traditional responsibilities from the family. No doubt the social studies will remains embroiled in controversy as long as they continue to deal with political, social, moral and religious questions.

Science

From a cursory look at the course offerings in the sciences at the secondary level, it would appear that little has changed in the last half century. General science is still a standard at the ninth grade, followed by biology, chemistry, and physics. A great deal has happened since Sputnik, however, with vast amounts of federal and foundation money going into the preparation of new materials for the teaching of science in U.S.A. at all levels. As with the social science curriculum reform movement, discovery and inductive approaches to the subject-matter have replaced the highly didactic approaches typical of the old science classrooms. Laboratory work has become increasingly important as high school students become involved in the actual work of scientists. Students conduct their own experiments and draw their own conclusions, rather than only observe demonstrations or read about the results of prior scientific research.

In addition to the "big three" science courses—biology, chemistry, and physics—earth science courses dealing with often-ignored aspects of geology, astronomy, and particularly ecology have become increasingly popular. In addition, science courses dealing with social and moral problems, often in an integrated approach using concepts from a variety of disciplines have been developed for high school use. Advanced placement courses for those with a scientific aptitude have been developed in many high schools along with special courses for the slow learner.

Mathematics

Mathematics instruction received much of the criticism of the secondary schools in the late 1950s. Like other areas of the secondary curriculum it received large amounts to develop new materials and approaches, and money to provide in-service training of teachers in the new mathematics. Most secondary schools still follow the traditional pattern of algebra in grade nine, plane geometry in grade ten, advanced algebra in grade eleven, followed by solid geometry and trigonometry in grade twelve. What occurs in these courses, however, changed greatly during the 1960s and 1970s, with much more emphasis upon discovery and enrichment programmes and an emphasis upon understanding, as opposed to the memorization of formulas and rules.

Many secondary schools moved beyond the traditional programmes and into the study of sets, elementary analysis, properties of the number system and the solution and graphical interpretation of algebraic inequalities. Much of the pressure has come from the changes in the elementary mathematics curriculum, where the "new math" has had a profound effect on what is taught and how it is learned. Many secondary schools set up advanced placement mathematics courses for which advanced students can receive college credit, in addition to introducing the use of individualized, programmed material, and the computer.

Fine Arts

Instrumental and vocal music enrolls millions of students at the secondary level and concerts by musical groups are attended by tens of millions. Emphasis upon performance skills is slowly giving way to the appreciation and enjoyment of music by all students, the vast majority of whom will never perform. Regrettably, many music teachers are frustrated performers, who see this as the basic goal of the music curriculum.

Art, like music, is an important part of our society, and as such, has a place in the curriculum. Along with music, however, art instruction in the past had been too often geared at producing great artists, rather than helping all people to enjoy a variety of art forms. The art curriculum today is crowded with drawing, painting, printing, sculpture, ceramics, and a host of other art forms.

Health and Physical Education

As with fine arts, physical educators have often seen their role as that of producing "professional" athletes, and judge the quality of their programmes on interscholastic win-loss records. Gradually, pressures have built up to get rid of the sexism in sports, with girls' athletic teams competing in many sports, and girls' sports becoming as extensive as the students: programme in many secondary schools. Intramural sports programmes and individual sports, which can be enjoyed throughout one's life have taken on increasing importance in the physical education programmes. Physical fitness, positive health habits and attitudes, and a variety of recreational skills have become basic objectives. Inordinate amounts of time and money are still being spent on students' football, cricket and basketball teams.

Vocational and Career Education

The government has encouraged the development of skill-oriented programmes to prepare secondary school students for the working world. Career education is a newer phenomenon, also being encouraged by the federal and many state governments, to help children in the elementary schools begin to get a feel for career opportunities, and then at the secondary level to actually experience time in a variety of occupational settings. With the increasing salaries of many of the "blue-collar" and office positions, the popularity of training programmes, either within the comprehensive secondary schools or in special technical-vocational schools, has rapidly improved.

Business education has gone beyond the old typing and secretarial skills and into such things as office management, marketing, data processing, and business law. Although practical arts in the form of "shop" and home economics still exist in most junior and many senior high schools, new programmes geared at seriously preparing young people for the working world have been developed in countless vocational areas. Aeronautics, air conditioning, refrigeration, audiovisual techniques, commercial art, electronics, painting and paper hanging, practical nursing, vocational horticulture, and photography are just a few of the fields which have been added to the traditional carpentry, auto mechanics, and agriculture curricula.

Every recent major national commission on the reform of secondary education has advocated that all students graduate with some saleable skill. Those that are going on to college may to need or use it immediately, but with the hundreds of thousands of unemployed liberal arts graduates from our nation's institutions of higher education, the future of vocational and technical programmes seems bright and secure.

***

13

Health Education and Medical Examination

School health education is a vital part of general education. It includes all such instruction that enlightens a student about activities and functions contributing to preservation, promotion and restoration of health. By means of a health education programme, the spread of diseases in the school going children can be checked and their eradication can also be attempted. A thorough knowledge of health rules underlines the needs of the study of anatomy and also the symptoms of common diseases of children. Practical knowledge of causes and diagnosis is equally essential. School health education also includes knowledge about the environment, equipments and routine of the schools as well.

Programme for Health

1. Health Appraisal or Medical Inspection.
2. Health Counselling and Follow-up.
3. Communicable Disease Control.
4. Emergency Care in Schools.
5. Identification and Education of the Handicapped Children.
6. Health of School Personnel.

Hygiene for All

Personal hygiene teaches the individual how to keep himself in health by paying attention to his cleanliness, exercise, rest and sleep, etc. The personal habits of an individual may be either important aids to the promotion of health and prolongation of life, or they may be powerful predisposing causes of disease. It is of the greatest importance to our well-being that we should form habits that are beneficial and not which as are hurtful to us.

Personal hygiene includes:

1. Cleanliness of the hair, the teeth, the nails, the eyes, the ears, etc.
2. Adequate rest and sleep.
3. Sound habits of bodily exercise.
4. Periodic medical check up every six or twelve months so that any disease may be detected at its very beginning and be properly treated before it has taken root.

Medical Test

Systematic medical examination in one of the most important means of taking care of the physical well-being of the students. Although this system has been in existence for many years, it has failed to achieve the desired results.

The Education Commission has observed the following defects in the prevailing system:

(i) It is done in a very superficial manner.

(ii) The remedial measures suggested are often not carried out.

(iii) Effective cooperation has not been established between the parents and the school authorities.

The Recommendations

Medical inspection to be effective should be done in the following manner:

1. It should be thorough and comprehensive and should not be treated as a mere routine. It should not merely concern itself with the height, weight and chest measurements but should also concern itself with ears, teeth, eyes, nose, heart and lungs etc. In fact no part of the body should be left unexamined as far as possible. The first inspection should be at the time of admission of the child in a school. If it is found out that the child is suffering from some chronic disease, he may be refused admission. Child should be examined every year. The last inspection will be just prior to leaving the school, which reveals the strength and weakness of the child and helps him to choose some vocation suited to his physical development also.

2. Remedial measures should be taken to remove defects.

3. Students with serious defects should be examined more frequently.

4. Three copies of the report should be prepared. One should be sent to the parents, another should be kept by the teacher-in-charge and the third one should be kept by the medical officer.

A few words may be said regarding 'follow-up' work. It has been rightly stated that medical inspection is of little or no use unless proper 'follow-up' work is undertaken. In many cases, it does not call for any extra burden. A slight care of the child brings about good results. The parents and the teachers should cooperate. Immediate action should be taken after the medical inspection is over. When the parents are unable to take remedial steps due to poverty, school should take upon itself the responsibility of looking after the health of the child. The State may arrange mobile hospital ambulances for the purpose. "In any case such remedial measures as the school medical officer may suggest should be adopted, and the school authorities should see that they are carried out," thus remarks the Education Commission.

Apart from medical inspection by the physician, daily inspection of the general cleanliness of the child should be made by the teacher. This costs nothing and can be made in a few minutes.

School Staff and Health of the Students

Personal Cleanliness. The daily morning inspection of the cleanliness of the students by the teacher is very helpful in enforcing personal cleanliness. A rapid survey of the class should be made. Competition may be introduced among the students. Cleanliness chart may be prepared and marks allotted to them.

Development of Habits Regarding Air. Stress should be laid on the need of fresh air at all times and especially while sleeping. The students should be asked not to cover their mouth at night. They should be taught to breathe through their noses.

Vaccination and Inoculation. At times of epidemics, precautionary measures should be suggested to them and they should be vaccinated and inoculated.

Training in First-aid Habits. The students should be instructed to give immediate attention to cuts and bruises.

Development of Habits of Hygienic Feeding. The students should be taught to take right type of food in a suitable quantity. They should be warned of the dangers of over-eating. They should be asked not to take sour food. The students should be made to understand the importance of drinking plenty of water.

Medical Inspection and Follow-up Work. Medical examination should be thorough and the follow-up work taken seriously.

Selection of Suitable Physical Exercises. A variety of physical activity programmes should exist in a school so that the students may choose activities to their linking.

Formation of Good Classroom Habits. A wise teacher would always pay due attention to the postures of the students. The students may be instructed to keep pens and pencils out of mouth and to use handkerchiefs when coughing. Such other matters should be attended to.

Particular Techniques

Apart from verbal talks, a good deal of health instruction can be imparted to the students in an interesting manner through the methods as suggested below:

Health Posters. Posters depicting washing of bodies, about various diseases like plague, malaria, etc., and about food, sleep and exercise etc., can be made and pasted on the school walls. Health authorities may be requested to supply these. Each poster should illustrate one idea only. Striking headings catch our attention. Students may be asked to help in preparing simple charts and posters.

Health Book. Each student should be asked to maintain a health book. One important health rule should be pasted on the top of each page. Pictures illustrating certain health rules may be pasted in it. It should also contain his health records.

Health Projects and Weeks. Once a year, a week may be set apart for the purpose of health education. Cleanliness campaigns in the school and locality go a long way in instilling ideas about health. Various committees of the students regarding different aspects of personal cleanliness, i.e. teeth, hair, nails, etc., may be formed. One teacher may serve as an adviser to each committee. The good posture committee should arrange posture competition and the participants should be asked to show proper posture. Prizes may be awarded to the best ones. Similarly, exercise competitions etc., may be arranged. Data regarding height, weight, chest measurements etc., may be collected by respective committees. Special lectures on general hygiene may be arranged.

Healthy Environment. Attempts should be made to make classrooms and the school building very attractive and conducive to health. This has a direct bearing on the child. As is the environment, so is the individual.

Excursions. 'Seeing is believing' is a true saying. Excursions to good dispensaries, water-supply centres, etc., may be planned for health educational purposes.

Film and Film Strips. Well-made health films and film strips are valuable in the teaching of health education.

Health Clubs. Like literary clubs, health clubs should be organized in schools. A definite weekly are monthly programme may be chalked out in cooperation with the Red Cross Society. Debates and declaimation contests on health matters may be arranged. Plays depicting health rules be staged.

Radio. Special programmes for children relating to health should be broadcast.

We may conclude by quoting the Education Commission, "This approach to the maintenance of school children's health may appear impracticable at first sight. But a clearer appreciation of the factors involved and a better coordination of the agencies concerned with the promotion of health will show that the adopting of such measures can produce tangible results within a reasonable time."

Health Counselling and Follow-up. The main aims of this service are:

1. Giving students the information about their health status as revealed by appraisal or medical inspection.
2. Motivating students to seek and accept needed treatment.
3. Acquainting parents with the significance of health problems and encouraging them to obtain needed care for their children.
4. Promoting each student's acceptance of responsibility for his own health in keeping with his stage of maturity.

Teachers, nurses and parents have to play an important role in the follow-up programme as actual improvement in the health of children depends more on follow-up than on any other school health activity.

Nutrition Problems

Importance of Nutritive and Balanced Diet. The quality and quantity of food taken by a person has an important bearing on his development. In fact nutritive and balanced diet provides the body with the required energy for doing everyday work.

Lack of Sufficient and Proper Food. When a person does not get proper food according to his age and nature of work, his health is adversely affected and malnutrition is caused.

Defective Atmosphere. Lack of fresh air, sunlight, physical exercise and unhealthy situations of school building also lead to malnutrition.

Over Work. Over work also adversely affects health.

Lack of Sleep. Lack of sleep also proves harmful for health.

Irregular Meals. Irregular and untimely eaten meals cause indigestion, dyspesia and constipation.

Physical Conditions

(i) Bad postures.

(ii) Laziness.

(iii) Pale and charmless face.

(iv) Drowsiness weight.

(v) Easily Fatigued.

(iv) Susceptibility to disease.

(vii) Under-weight

Mental Conditions

(i) Gloomy nature.

(ii) Unenthusiasm.

(iii) Lack of concentration.

(iv) Slow comprehension.

(v) Forgetful memory.

(iv) Irritability.

Why School Meals. It is now generally recognized that in the wake of under-nutrition and malnutrition of the most of the Indian children, the school must take up the responsibility to make up this deficiency. This will not only assist in improving the health and physical development of the child but also assist him in making quicker and sounder progress in his studies because a child who is better-fed and healthier makes rapid progress. It is, therefore, essential that we must develop a universal programme of school meals as an integral part of its programme of universal, free and compulsory primary education.

Free Milk. With the help of United Nations International Children's Emergency Fund (UNICEF), which gave milk powder free of charge, milk was distributed to primary school children.

Storage, Preparation and Distribution Arrangement. It must be stressed that food should be prepared and served under proper-hygienic conditions. There should be adequate storage facilities and also adequate space for feeding of children.

Assistance of the Central Government. In order to assist the development of the programme, the Government of India approved a centrally sponsored scheme of grand-in-aid to State Governments in 1962-63. Under this scheme, assistance is offered to State Governments to the extent of one-third of the total expenditure incurred by them in school feeding programmes.

Subsidy by the Government. The Committee recommended that the Government should support the school meal programme besides the contribution of the community at the rate of 50 per cent of the total cost.

Supply of Gift Food. The Mid-day Meals programme known as Nutritional Support to Primary Education was launched on August 15, 1995 on a nation-wide scale.

The Gestures

We can hardly ignore the seriousness of poor postures. It affects health, physical efficiency, mental attitude and appearance of an individual. Most of our diseases are the outcome of poor postures. A teacher can do much in the classroom work and physical instruction period to prevent bad postural habits in the students. As a result of poor postures says Dr. Mosher; "constipation, diarrhoea, flatulence, disturbance of the circulation, nervous irritability and, most marked of all fatigue out of proportion to the effort expended lessen the efficiency of the individual and often make life a burden." Some of the main defects of poor postures are given below:

(i) Interfere in the normal working of respiration, circulation and digestion.

(ii) Badly affect the eyesight.

(iii) Develop crooked bodies which are not normal in shape, and look very unpleasant.

(iv) Lead to round shoulders and drooping body.

(v) Decrease physical efficiency and develop laziness.

(vi) Spoil handwriting because the students will not be able to hold the pen properly.

(vii) Result in undesirable traits, *e.g.*, timidness, lack of courage, etc.

The Reasons

(a) Weakness of the muscles which may be due to lack of exercise.

(b) Wrong postural habits due to lack of information regarding correct position.

(c) Wrong writing positions.

(d) Defective desks and seats compelling the students to stretch or cramp their bodies.

(e) Illegible writing of the teacher on the blackboard.

(f) Illness of the students.

(g) Wrong reading positions.

(h) Defective eyesight.

(i) Wrong postures of the teachers leading to depressing effects on the students.

(j) Defective hearing.

(k) Wrong type of dress of the students.

Various Categories

(i) Standing postures.

(ii) Sitting postures.

(iii) Writing postures.

(iv) Reading postures.

(v) Walking postures.

Corrective Measures

(i) The student should be asked to take regular exercise to strengthen muscles.

(ii) Suitable furniture should be provided.

(iii) Stools should be provided for smaller children so that they may learn to sit without reclining against the chair.

(iv) Good postural habits should be developed. The students should be told that the head, neck, trunk, thigh and legs are in a straight line in a good standing posture. While writing, the students should be asked to keep their note-books at a distance of one foot. While reading, the books should be held vertically so that the top and the bottom of the books are at an equal distance from the eyes. The distance of 12 inches is an ideal one.

(v) Suitable corrective postural exercises should be recommended to the students.

(vi) Students having defective eyesight and hearing should be seated on the front benches.

(vii) Bold type books should be selected.

(viii) The aid of school medical officer should be sought.

(ix) Rooms should be suitably ventilated and sufficient accommodation should be provided.

HEALTH EXAMINATION AND MEDICAL INSPECTION

Provisions for medical examinations of school children were among the first health measures to receive legal sanction, although the importance of these measures was barely recognized until the second decade of the present century. These laws vary widely in the different states, some mandatory requiring health examinations at periodic intervals others permissive enabling state and local boards of education to require such examinations as may be desired. Either the education department or health department may be charged with the responsibility of administering the examinations, or joint action is sometimes indicated.

Usually the term "examine" is restricted to functions performed by physicians and dentists. Nurses and teachers "inspect" children. Frequently the line of demarcation between examination and inspection is difficult to determine.

Where legislation is contemplated dealing with the health examinations of school children, perhaps the following items will prove helpful:

1. The law should be mandatory in indicating the governmental organization (board of education or board of health) responsible for setting the standards used.

2. The minimum number of examinations during the public school life of the child should be stated, together with the minimum list of items to be covered, with no limit restricting the optimum number of items or thoroughness of the examination.
3. Provisions should be made for a coordinated report of physical and mental examinations (the latter performed by adequately trained personnel), and for the use of these coordinated reports in improving the educational guidance of children.
4. The law should stipulate that all teachers be trained to detect the signs of communicable disease and of gross physical defects.

Vaccination. Great variation exists among the several states in the legal provisions dealing with vaccination. A few state laws prohibit compulsory vaccination. In other states, boards of health may adopt such measures for general vaccination as are deemed proper and necessary. In other states, health authorities may insist on vaccination if smallpox shows a tendency to become epidemic. The laws or regulations in some states specifically require vaccination for school attendance; occasionally this provision applies to both teachers and children.

Many judicial decisions of the courts uphold the requirements of general compulsory vaccination when deemed necessary by the board of health, except in the few states where requirements are prohibited by law.

School Plants

Regulations of the state education department, that have the effect of laws, of an establish the requirement of size, location, and suitability of school grounds. In addition to grounds, regulations may provide standards for the construction, remodeling, and sanitation of schools.

Most states have laws requiring the use of fire-proof materials in the construction of school buildings, although many school plants are fire traps of the worst kind.

The laws in many states specify ventilation standards based upon old and faulty notions of air conditioning. Despite more than a half-century of accumulated knowledge, these archaic laws remain on the statutes. During the latter part of the 19th century it was believed that the carbon dioxide in expired air was a menace to health. In response to this belief laws were passed requiring a stipulated amount of fresh air per minute for each child in occupied classrooms. Although later, scientists proved that the factors of movement and temperature are more significant in maintaining health than the chemical composition of air, few new laws were passed. Most of the old ones, however, remain on the books even though they are ignored.

Health Instruction

Most states have laws, which require the teaching of physiology and hygiene. Every state requires instruction on the deleterious effects of alcohol and arcotics, with tobacco mentioned in several of these statutes. In some states the legislators even went so far as to indicate that textbooks in physiology and hygiene shall devote a specified proportion of the book, or a definite number of pages, to the effects of alcohol and narcotics.

Legislation or state education department regulations on health instruction may establish this programme as a special subject, combine it with physiology and hygiene or include it with physical education. Such legislation or regulations often prescribe: (1) the use of textbooks; (2) grades in which instruction shall be given; (3) the number of minutes per week to be devoted to the subject, and (4) suggestions as to method.

Is State Legislation Needed? It is impossible to answer this question with any degree of assurance due to the conflicting evidence given by those in positions of administrative authority. Probably the majority of opinion would favour some sort of legislation, either specially, or by mention of health and physical education in the more general statute which enumerates the subjects which may or must be taught.

Under the philosophy that pervades modern social theory, a state is consciously aware of its constituents, and to assure itself of advancement accepts as one of its: responsibilities the provision of equalized educational opportunities. Hence, laws and regulations are passed requiring all local districts to comply with certain minimum standards compatible with the best interests of the state as a whole.

The pace of education is set by the tread of the backward communities. Therefore, it is the duty of the state to indicate through laws and regulations the speed of the educational activities of these communities. On the other hand, the state must ever be an incentive to better districts, encouraging them in their efforts to improve the educational offering. Legislation, regulations and an enlightened public go hand in hand, occasionally one precedes the other, but in the final analysis all are essential.

Conflicts between Local Agencies. Conflict in the administration of play and recreation in municipalities is real and its by-products hurtful to the program. Local municipal authorities with budgets and patronage to dispense compete for the right to serve children. As a result, some communities possess two sets of play-grounds, two sets of equipment and facilities, and two staffs. This duplication is wasteful of tax money, produces conflicts between and makes rivals of local officials, and contributes nothing to the object of all their endeavors—the education and welfare of children and adults.

The lack of uniformity and orderly planning for play and recreation is due largely to the Topsy-like character of urban growth and legislative development. Municipal functions and responsibilities have increased without master plans that might have brought efficient and more useful service to the community.

The legal aspects of the conflict add to the difficulties. In states with genuine home rule provisions, cities may determine freely the condition under which recreation shall be conducted. Some states have passed laws specifically dealing with recreation. But in most cities the board of education is locally elected and in some appointed by the local city government. This has serious political relationships. A city government operating usually under the emblem of a political party, often makes its decisions with respect to political advantage, and frequently conducts its administration to strengthen its political future quite regardless of recognized principles of orderly and progressive administration.

A Cooperative Plan. There is one way out of the difficulty. This is a cooperative arrangement between the board of education and the city government with respect to the administration of play and recreation in the community.

The same sort of cooperative action sometimes is established in health service. Where the state law requires the board of health to responsible for the health of children, it is impossible for the board-to—delegate its authority to school physicians, for in law a delegated authority cannot be re-delegated. The board of health cooperating with the board of education, however, can appoint jointly with the board of education the same person to conduct the health service in the schools.

In similar fashion the city government and the board of education may unite in the selection of one executive officer to administer the physical education activities of school children and the recreational and developmental activities of preschool and adult groups on city parks or school properties. Less complete integration can be secured by an agreement with respect to the use of facilities, but the larger values of unified administration favor one executive officer.

Legal Provisions Necessary. In cities with home rule rights, the joint action indicated above is easily possible, although legal difficulties would be prevented by the passage of an enabling act by the legislature granting to proper local authorities the right to spend tax money for recreational purposes. In many states the school law restricts the powers of the board of education to the legal sessions of the school term, hence the board of education is unable to provide money for recreational purposes after the school day is closed or during vacation periods. In. numerous states such power is assumed under the broad provisions of home rule charters that give the local government considerable freedom. In some states governmental authorities assert that no such power of boards exists.

Boards of education are regarded as quasi-corporations charge with governmental functions. As such they are not liable for injuries caused by the negligence of agents, although boards are liable for their own-negligence. In this case, negligence must be proved, and depends largely on defects of construction of facilities or defects in maintenance which have been reported by the person in charge to the board which is responsible for keeping the facilities in good repair.

In legal parlance the question of conducting an "attractive nuisance" poses a complex problem. Gymnasium and playground apparatus attracts children who may be injured in using' these facilities unless proper supervision is provided. Lawful use of such apparatus in regularly scheduled physical education classes, and during recess periods, does not constitute a nuisance per se, provided adequate supervision is available. The doctrine of "attractive nuisance" does apply when 'such facilities are used by children who trespass in playing on the apparatus at times when school is not legally in session.

When fees are charged for the use of facilities, or for attendance as spectators, a different situation arises with reference' to the liability of boards of education. If the activity is provided for the sole benefit of the public, and not for profit to the municipality, the board of education usually is not liable even though a small charge is made to help pay current expenses. If, however, such property is maintained primarily as a source of revenue, and a person is injured either as a participant or spectator, the municipality is liable.

Since the liability of boards of education so frequently remains in doubt due to varying state legislation and to the exigencies of particular situations, it is recommended that legal council advise the board concerning the establishment of appropriate policies and procedures to protect the safety of persons who is school facilities.

***

Index

R

S

T

U

W